Time I Am - ı

To Save Time

Is To

Lengthen Life

By
Dr. Sahadeva dasa

B.com., FCA., AICWA., PhD
Chartered Accountant

Soul Science University Press

www.TimeIAm.com

Readers interested in the subject matter of this
book are invited to correspond with the publisher at:
SoulScienceUniversity@gmail.com   +91 98490 95990
or visit DrDasa.com

First Edition: February 2014

Soul Science University Press expresses its gratitude to the
Bhaktivedanta Book Trust International (BBT), for the use of quotes by
His Divine Grace A.C.Bhaktivedanta Swami Prabhupada.

ISBN 978-93-82947-07-3

Published by:
Dr. Sahadeva dasa for Soul Science University Press

Printed by:
Rainbow Print Pack, Hyderabad

To order a copy write to purnabramhadasa@gmail.com
or buy online: Amazon.com, rlbdeshop.com

By The Same Author

Oil-Final Countdown To A Global Crisis And Its Solutions

End of Modern Civilization And Alternative Future

To Kill Cow Means To End Human Civilization

Cow And Humanity - Made For Each Other

Cows Are Cool - Love 'Em!

Let's Be Friends - A Curious, Calm Cow

Wondrous Glories of Vraja

We Feel Just Like You Do

Tsunami Of Diseases Headed Our Way - Know Your Food Before Time Runs Out

Cow Killing And Beef Export - The Master Plan To Turn India Into A Desert By 2050

Capitalism Communism And Cowism - A New Economics For The 21st Century

Noble Cow - Munching Grass, Looking Curious And Just Hanging Around

World - Through The Eyes Of Scriptures

An Inch of Time Can Not Be Bought With A Mile of Gold

Life Is Nothing But Time - Time Is Life, Life Is Time

Lost Time Is Never Found Again

Spare Us Some Carcasses - An Appeal From The Vultures

Cow Dung - A Down-To- Earth Solution To Global Warming And Climate Change

Cow Dung For Food Security And Survival of Human Race

(More information on availability on DrDasa.com)

Contents

The Author

Preface

Time is our most precious resource. All we have in life is time. We have to wake up before it's too late. Often, we realize the importance of time only when there is little of it left. Our greatest capital asset is our unexpired years of productive life.

We can not influence the supply of this resource called time. C.S. Lewis says, "The future is something which everyone reaches at the rate of sixty minutes an hour, whatever he does, whoever he is."

This realization is not very easy to come by. It is said that a wise person does at once, what a fool does at last. Both do the same thing; only at different times.

Henry Twells laments the passing away of time, "When as a child I laughed and wept, time crept. When as a youth I waxed more bold, time strolled. When I became a full-grown man, time RAN. When older still I daily grew, time FLEW. Soon I shall find, in passing on, time gone."

So the bad news is time flies. But the good news is you're the pilot. If you want, you can steer the plane of your life. Fortunate are the ones who stand forewarned. Because forewarned is forearmed. Charles Richards finally has a piece of advice, "Don't be fooled by the calendar. There are only as many days in the year as you make use of. One man gets only a week's value out of a year while another man gets a full year's value out of a week. "

Sahadeva dasa

Dr. Sahadeva dasa
1st February 2014
Secunderabad, India

A Note On The Book Format

This book is based on One Victory A Day™ format. The chapters are arranged date wise. A reader need not read the book serially. He can open any chapter and he will find something useful for the day.

According to surveys, 80% of the books bought don't get read beyond 10% of their contents. They just sit in the shelves. This is especially true in recent times.

The thickness of the book acts as a deterrent, especially due to lack of time. Desperation grows and book lands in the shelf.

In One Victory A Day™ format, the book need not be completed. The idea is to read the chapter related to the day, and then understand, digest, assimilate and implement the information. That is improving life in small measures or changing life one day at a time. Throughout the day, you can try to reflect on and implement the newfound information.

Most of the books bought are not read fully because the reader can not relate the information to his or her life. Purpose of knowledge is not entertainment but betterment of life. Purpose of information is transformation, otherwise it's a waste of time.

Ingestion of information without assimilation is like intake of food without digestion.

To scale a highrise, we go up one step at a time. To finish our meal, we eat one morsel at a time. A skyscraper is constructed one brick at a time. And an ocean is nothing but an assembly of many drops. This is the power of small. A big target, when broken down into small steps, becomes easily attainable.

People who are not into reading should cultivate the habit of reading in small installments. Phenomenal achievements can be accomplished by consistent and daily improvements. Good reading is as essential as clean air and water. Anything we do regularly becomes a habit.

The mind's garden will produce whatever we sow in it. Daily we are being bombarded with a massive dose of undesirable information. The only way to counteract it is through assimilation of desirable information.

Time

What is time? The question has perplexed philosophers since, well, time began. If you want to give a quick answer, you might say, "Time is a series of passing moments." Or you might want to go for a more complex answer, "Time is the basic measurement of change which is astronomically and mathematically calculated in relation to the speed, transformation or life of a particular object."

In other words, time is the basic measurement by which we calculate past, present and future. Modern science as well as various traditions have defined time. In Hebrew literature time is accepted, as a representation of God. It is stated therein: "God, who at sundry times and in diverse manners spake in time past unto the fathers by the prophets...." In the same spirit, Vedic tradition explains time to be another feature of God: "My Lord, I consider Your Lordship to be eternal time, the supreme controller, without beginning and end, the all-pervasive one. *(Srimad Bhagavatam 1.8.28)*

In the Bhagavad-gita, Lord Krsna gives His own answer in a few words. "Time I am," He says, "the great destroyer of the worlds."

kalah kalayatam aham
Among subduers I am time ~ *Bhagavad-gita 10.30*

Time thus is an inconceivable energy of the Supreme Lord through which He ultimately destroys everything.

Time has long been a major subject of study in religion, philosophy, and science, but defining it in a manner applicable to all fields without circularity has consistently eluded scholars. Nevertheless, diverse fields such as business, industry, sports, the sciences, and the performing arts all incorporate some notion of time into their respective measuring systems.

Two contrasting viewpoints on time divide many prominent philosophers. One view is that time is part of the fundamental structure of the universe—a dimension independent of events, in which events occur in sequence. Sir Isaac Newton subscribed to this realist view, and hence it is sometimes referred to as Newtonian time.

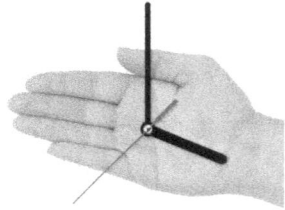

The opposing view is that time does not refer to any kind of "container" that events and objects "move through", nor to any entity that "flows", but that it is instead part of a fundamental intellectual structure (together with space and number) within which humans sequence and compare events. This second view, in the tradition of

> *Material nature itself is constituted by three qualities: the mode of goodness, the mode of passion and the mode of ignorance. Above these modes there is eternal time, and by a combination of these modes of nature and under the control and purview of eternal time there are activities, which are called karma.*
>
> *Out of these five, the Lord, the living entities, material nature and time are eternal.*
>
> *So the Lord, the living entity, material nature and time are all interrelated and are all eternal. However, the other item, karma, is not eternal.*
>
> ~ Srila Prabhupada (Bhagavad gita - Introduction)

Gottfried Leibniz and Immanuel Kant, holds that time is neither an event nor a thing, and thus is not itself measurable nor can it be travelled.

References:

Rynasiewicz, Robert : Johns Hopkins University (12 August 2004). "Newton's Views on Space, Time, and Motion"

Burnham, Douglas : Staffordshire University (2006). "Gottfried Wilhelm Leibniz (1646–1716) Metaphysics – 7. Space, Time, and Indiscernibles"

Measurement Of Time

We measure time in terms of the movements of physical objects. The time the earth takes to orbit the sun we call a year. The time the moon takes to orbit the earth we call a month. And the time the earth takes to revolve on its axis we call a day. To further subdivide our days into hours, minutes, and seconds we observe the movements of other physical objects. Sand, water, pendulums, quartz crystals, and cesium atoms are a few of the things man has used to make his timepieces. By observing how many times these objects swing, rotate, vibrate, and so on during the greater movements of the planets, we can subdivide our days.

In fact, every physical object or mechanism is a clock of sorts, because everything physical is affected by time. Even the beating of our hearts and the gradual decay of our bodies can serve to measure the passing moments.

Time is one of the seven fundamental physical quantities in the International System of Units. Time is used to define other quantities—such as velocity—so defining time in terms of such quantities would result in circularity of definition. An operational definition of time, wherein one says that observing a certain number of repetitions of one or another standard cyclical event (such as the passage of a free-swinging pendulum) constitutes one standard unit such as the second, is highly useful in the conduct of both advanced experiments and everyday affairs of life.

Temporal measurement of time has occupied scientists and technologists, and was a prime motivation in navigation and astronomy. Currently, the international unit of time, the second, is defined in terms of radiation emitted by caesium atoms. Time is also of significant social importance, having economic value ("time is money") as well as personal value, due to an awareness of the limited time in each day and in human life spans.

Temporal measurement, or chronometry, takes two distinct period forms: the calendar, a mathematical abstraction for calculating extensive periods of time and the clock, a physical mechanism that counts the ongoing passage of time. In day-to-day life, the clock is consulted for periods less than a day, the calendar, for periods longer than a day. Increasingly, personal electronic devices display both calendars and clocks simultaneously.

References:

Duff, Okun, Veneziano, p. 3.

The Two Faces of Time, Mathuresa dasa

Carrol, Sean, Chapter One, Section Two, Plume, 2010. From Eternity to Here.

Richards, E. G. (1998). Mapping Time: The Calendar and its History. Oxford University Press. pp. 3–5

Our duration of life is measured, and no one is able to enhance it even by a second against the scheduled time ordained by the supreme will. Such valuable time, especially for the human being, should be cautiously spent because even a second passed away imperceptibly cannot be replaced, even in exchange for thousands of golden coins amassed by hard labor. Every second of human life is meant for making an ultimate solution to the problems of life,

~ Srila Prabhuapada (Srimad Bhagavatam 1.13.17)

January 3

The Wheel Of Time

The Wheel of time or wheel of history (Kalachakra) is a concept found in several religious traditions and philosophies, notably religions of Indian origin such as Hinduism and Buddhism, which regard time as cyclical and consisting of repeating ages. Many other cultures contain belief in a similar concept: notably, the Q'ero Indians in Peru, Hopi Indians of Arizona and Incan, Mayan and few other tribes.

Peter Lynds has put forward a cosmology model in which time is cyclic and the universe repeats exactly an infinite number of times. Because it is exactly the same cycle that repeats, Lynds argues that this resolves a number of thorny issues in cosmology.

The Sanskrit word kala-chakra denotes time's control of the cyclical movement of the physical world. Kala is a name for the Supreme Person in His feature as time, and chakra means "wheel." Each and every physical thing, from the smallest atomic particle up to the complete form of the universe, has a particular wheel of time that it is obliged to follow. Kala-chakra therefore refers not only to an object's movements but to its overall duration -- its life expectancy -- as well. The earth, sun, moon, stars, planets, our physical bodies, and so on disappear in the course of time, and their particular durations are all kala-chakras.

All our analysis and measurement, however, does not make time any less perplexing or any more perceivable. What we perceive in the movement and change of the innumerable clocks -- man-made and natural -- that surround us is not time, but time's effect on these objects. And what we are measuring is also not time, but the duration of these effects in relation to each other. Time itself is immeasurable, having no beginning or end. It stands above all relative effects, employing its various chakras to shape the physical world according to the Lord's will.

But although we cannot observe time directly, we can learn much -- with the help of the Vedic literature -- by observing time's effects. Krsna says that as time He is "the great destroyer of the worlds." And yet, as we can understand from the Vedic texts as well as from our own experience, time brings not only destruction but creation and sustenance as well.

Within every kala-chakra there is a point of creation, a point of sustenance, and a point of destruction. Everything has its given schedule of creation, sustenance, and destruction under the influence of time. The universe itself, according to the Srimad-Bhagavatam, is created at a certain time, sustained for the equivalent of 310 trillion

The sun who is the king of all the planets, full of infinite effulgence, the image of the good soul, is as the eye of this world. I adore the primeval Lord Govinda in pursuance of whose order the sun performs his journey mounting the wheel of time.
~ Brahma Samhita 5.52

solar years, and then destroyed. After destruction, time brings about recreation, and the cycle begins again. Thus, although the overall effect is destruction, the physical world goes through repeated creations and annihilations.

Within these cycles of creation and annihilation, time has many other manifestations. Time brings birth, death, old age, and disease -- the fourfold miseries of material life mentioned in the Gita. It also brings on miseries caused by natural disasters like hurricanes, tornadoes, droughts, and so on, as well as miseries caused by the attacks of other living creatures, like insects or our human enemies.

All in all, therefore, time as we know it is a vehicle of suffering. It surrounds us, imprisons us, and gradually destroys everything we have. The pleasure we do experience is sure to have an end and sure to be mixed with suffering. This is like the pleasure of eating ice cream mixed with sand: the overall effect is misery.

References:

Mathuresa Dasa, The Two Faces Of Time

"Time". The American Heritage Dictionary of the English Language (Fourth ed.) (Houghton Mifflin Company). 2011.

Linear Time

In general, the Judeo-Christian concept, based on the Bible, is that time is linear, beginning with the act of creation by God. The general Christian view is that time will end with the end of the world.

A Major Feature Of Western Cultural World-View

Linear time is a major feature of Western cultural world-view, apparently initiated by Newton some 300 years ago. It portrays time as an absolute physical reality, and says that the passage of time is independent of consciousness. So it doesn't matter what you think, feel, or do, or how you look at time, time doesn't change as a result.

Of course clock time is a standard that we don't want to change: its continuous measurement of the passage of events enables us to coordinate our activities. But linear time, which is an experiential perspective completely independent of clock time, combines (1) the actual feeling of time slipping from one moment to another, and (2) many different feelings--like overwhelm, pressure, anxiety, hurry, time poverty, frustration, and boredom--that we have as and about time.

In the linear view, time flows like a conveyor belt that moves horizontally from past to present to future at the same unchangeable speed for all of us. Time feels out of our control; we may feel some helplessness, and think we can only adapt to this 'reality'.

The conveyor passes through three rooms: past, present, and future. We're always in the present room--we take that for granted. We can't go into the future or past rooms because there seems to be an impenetrable divider between the rooms.

On the conveyor there is an apparently endless series of containers extending into the past on the one hand and into the future on the other. The way we 'spend our time' is by putting our activities into the containers as the conveyor moves by us. These containers are all the same size, so we can put only so many activities in a given container, then that time is used up, and the container moves into the past. What was put into the containers moves farther and farther into the past, and doesn't seem to affect us.

Wasting time is not filling the containers as they go by. Since we know that there are a limited number of containers that will pass by during our lifetime, we're anxious about not having enough time. Furthermore, since each container has the same size, what we can accomplish in any time period appears to be limited by the structure of time itself. Racing

against the conveyor and trying to overfill containers can lead to overwhelm and burnout.

The dividers between the past, present, and future rooms have hazy windows in them. Even though we can't go into the future room, we can look into it through its window. Planning an activity is similar to peering through the hazy window to see how the fuzzy future forms might shape up. We then get an idea of what's 'coming down the pike' toward us on the conveyor.

With the experience of time flowing between past, present, and future there is a dissatisfied self 'spending time' in the foreground. The self reaches out for satisfaction, looking to other people to fulfill desires, or seeking out special things and activities.

References:

Steve Randall, Ph.D, 1996

Edward T. Hall, The Dance of Life (New York: Doubleday, 1983), pp. 78-9.

http://www.manage-time.com/linear.html

A body is given to us by the superior power, and the duration of life is also fixed up. Even the greatest scientist, he cannot increase a moment's time for his life. That is not possible. A moment's life. Professor Einstein was a great scientist, but he could not find out any means that instead of living for, say, eighty years, he could live eighty years, one day. No, that is not possible. That is not possible. Your destiny, duration of life—fixed up. And how it is fixed up? The machine is breathing. Machine is breathing. Just like the clock goes on, tick-tick, tick-tick, tick-tick. As soon as the tick-tick stops, then whole things is lost.

Similarly, our breathing is going on, tick-tick, tick-tick, tick-tick, a fixed time. Just like you wind your clock, so that winding will help, tick-tick, for a certain duration of time, say, twenty-four hours. Similarly, there is winding in our life, a spring. That "tick-tick" means this breathing.

~ Srila Prabhupada (Lecture, Srimad Bhagavatam 1.16.24 -- Hawaii, January 20, 1974)

Time Is Money

And Much More...

I have all the time in the world, but I do not have all the money in the world. Time can be spent, wasted, earned, and ignored. Same goes for money.

Most people look at their bank accounts with great attention and assess how much money they have to spend, to invest, and to give away... but, they don't look at their time the same way, and end up wasting this incredibly valuable resource. In fact, time is much more valuable than money because

> So we should not waste our time, a single moment. Time is very valuable. In your country, they say, "Time is money." So either you take money, that is artha, or paramartha. Money is required in the material world, and in spiritual world, paramartha, spiritual asset. Some way or other, even those who are materialists, they do not waste their time. So we are after spiritual realization. How we can waste our time? Time is very valuable. So we should not waste time.
>
> ~ Srila Prabhupada (Lecture, The Nectar of Devotion, Vrindavan, October 24, 1972)

you can use your time to make money, but you can't use money to purchase more time.

You can get more money, but you cannot get more time. With money, you can buy a clock, but not time. Time begets money but not vise versa.

Each day has only 24 hours – nobody has any more than anyone else.

"Time is money - order more clocks."

Everyone, from a pauper to president, fills those hours, one after the other, until they are all filled up. Every single minute is unique, and once gone, can never be regained.

When you look at someone who has accomplished a lot, you can be pretty sure that he or she has spent considerable amounts of time mastering the required skills, filling hours upon hours with hard work. There are those who look at others' accomplishments and say, "I had that idea, " or "I could have done that." But ideas are cheap and intentions are just that. If you don't invest the time needed to achieve those goals then all you have are empty ambitions.

Reference:
Matt Harvey, December 2010

Trading Time

For Money

It is understood that we need money to survive. In a world where nothing is free for the taking, everyone needs to make money in order to live. As such, people stress over money – worry about things that would help them make more money. However, we forget that there is something far more important than cold-hard cash, and that's the time we have to live.

Far too much emphasis is put on money in today's world. We forget the real treasures of life are mostly things that don't cost a thing.

The error is in the belief that more money will buy one even greater time... But it rarely does. It's clearly observed that the more you have, the more you are slave to what you have. Just ask any millionaire.

> *Therefore if you have spoiled that point of time without any utility, then you have spent at least many millions of dollars for nothing. That should be our calculation. ayusah ksana eko 'pi na labhyah svarna-kotibhih, na cen nirarthakam nitih. If that valuable time is spoiled without any benefit, then just imagine how much you are losing every moment. So we should be very careful about our time. Don't spoil time. That is our request. Don't spoil time like animals.*
> *~ Srila Prabhupada (Lecture -- New York, April 16, 1969)*

Sure, money can buy you a host of things and facilities, but often these are just distractions. Comfort is not the same as happiness.

We should realize that all dreams have a common thread- time: When I just get enough time, I'm going to… After just one more thousand…But as Sterling Hayden Once observed: "To be truly rewarding, a voyage, like a life, must be based on a firm foundation of financial unrest… Which shall it be, bankruptcy of purse, or bankruptcy of spirit?"

You need not spend 'all' your time trying to make money. Why? That's because they print more everyday and it will always be in supply. No matter what you do, money will be everywhere and there will be plenty of chances for you to get some. However, as for time, you only have now. You cannot gain back time that you have lost, so now is the time for you to take your chances!

MY DAD SAYS TIME IS MONEY, SO HOW MANY LOLLIPOPS CAN I GET FOR ELEVEN THIRTY?

The focus should never be on the money, but rather the things money could achieve. Once you see clearly that money is just a means to an end, but not the end itself, a whole world of possibility opens up, and a great weight is lifted: Money is only an obstacle, a waypoint, on the path to the real goal. It's a distraction. The shortest distance between two points is a straight line, and the surest path to your dreams is always a direct one.

Some of the poorest countries have some of the happiest people. Ever notice that often the less people have, the happier they are? Why is that? Perhaps it is true that "Freedom is just another word for 'nothing left to lose".

There is a high spiritual price to pay for financial gain, pretty much across the board, yet we all rush headlong into it regardless.

Finally, your bank balance at the time of death represents the work that was not needed at all.

References:

Chris Carpenter's Life Hacks

http://goodinformations.wordpress.com/

Boyle, David (2006). The Little Money Book. The Disinformation Company.

David Graeber (2001). Toward an anthropological theory of value: the false coin of our own dreams. Palgrave Macmillan.

Cash Rich

And Time Poor

Money-rich, time-poor is an expression which arose in Britain at the end of the 20th century to describe groups of people who, whilst having a high disposable income through well-paid employment, had relatively little leisure time as a result.

The phrase is still in use. Time poverty has also been coined as a noun for the phenomenon.

Many people accept time poverty as a necessary condition of employment; others have sought to solve the problem through downshifting or accepting simple life.

> *Because our time is very valuable. If we want to utilize our short duration of life which we have got at our disposal, we must utilize it for self-realization, not for unnecessarily increasing the necessities of bodily wants. This is not a good type of civilization, simply wasting time for sense gratification. Time should be utilized for greater advantage. Chanakya Pandita says that ayusah ksana eno 'pi na labhyah svarna-kotibhih. You know... In your country I have seen many tabloids, "Time is money." Yes, actually time is very valuable, but we do not know how to utilize this time. That is the mistake of this present civilization. Time should not be, I mean to say, wasted simply for sense gratification. So far the problem of sense gratification is there, it should be minimized. It should not be increased.*
> *~ Srila Prabhupada, (Srimad-Bhagavatam 5.5.1-2 -- London, September 13, 1969)*

It is often believed that the quality of our life can be evaluated based on two essential commodities, the amount of income we earn and the amount of free time we have left over after working to generate that income. Several time-use researchers and economists have emphasized the importance of free time when considering the quality of a person's life.

Bittman & Matheson (1999) emphasized the importance of free time as follows; "The ability to participate in social life is the product of both access to leisure goods and services, and a sufficient quality of leisure time." Harvey (1996), a Canadian economist having lead the International Association for Time Use Research, concluded that "time poor people realize less household production, as the result of their time deficit, have to substitute these`missing' products and services by market products and services."

Are You Time Poor?

Do you...
- Constantly feel rushed
- Feel like there's too much to do
- Have trouble sleeping
- Take few breaks or holidays
- Have little unscheduled/unstructured time
- Feel stressed out
- Feel worn out/exhausted
- Have the sense that your days fly by quickly ("It's March already?!")

If so, you may be suffering from time poverty.

References:

Are People Money Rich And Time Poor In Japan?, Masago Fujiwara, Michinori Hirata

Time Poverty: The Cost Of Being Money Rich And Time Poor, Nelly Uhlenkott March 2012

Time Poverty

In A Century of Progress

At the dawn of the twentieth century, people saw great hope in technological innovations to make their life easier. Saving people's time was the professed goal of these innovations.

But here we are, busier than ever before and suffering from acute time poverty.

Modern conveniences and fast food haven't seemed to help. Instead of having more free time, we've become more efficient at everyday activities, which has allowed us to pack even more into our schedules. More and more, people are multitasking and running straight from one activity to another with no break in between.

"I'd like to schedule a time-management seminar on my calendar...as soon as I can find time to buy a calendar!"

Technology can be incredibly useful, but it can also put the pressure on to fill any free moment with tasks and to be contactable during all our waking hours by text, phone, or email.

What's the Big Deal About Being Time Poor?

Being time poor can decrease your quality of life. People who are time poor often say that they feel perpetually stressed out, tired, and unfulfilled. Time poverty can have negative effects on your physical, mental and emotional health, as well as your sense of self and meaning in life. It can also can also lead to strained relationships with your romantic partner, your friends, and your family.

Being time poor is a common ailment, but also a very serious one. Increasing for time wealth can lead to dramatic improvements in your life satisfaction, health and sense of wellbeing.

References:

Time Poverty: The Cost Of Being Money Rich And Time Poor, Nelly Uhlenkott March 2012

Charlie Gere, (2005) Art, Time and Technology: Histories of the Disappearing Body, Berg

Most often, those who work very hard day and night to clear the burden of self-created duties say that they have no time to hear of the immortality of the living being. To such mud has, material gains, which are destructible, are life's all in all—despite the fact that the mud has enjoy only a very small fraction of the fruit of labor. Sometimes they spend sleepless days and nights for fruitive gain, and although they may have ulcers or indigestion, they are satisfied with practically no food; they are simply absorbed in working hard day and night for the benefit of illusory masters. Ignorant of their real master, the foolish workers waste their valuable time serving mammon. Unfortunately, they never surrender to the supreme master of all masters, nor do they take time to hear of Him from the proper sources. The swine who eat the night soil do not care to accept sweetmeats made of sugar and ghee. Similarly, the foolish worker will untiringly continue to hear of the sense-enjoyable tidings of the flickering mundane world, but will have very little time to hear about the eternal living force that moves the material world.

~ Srila Prabhupada (Bhagavad Gita 7.15)

Invaluable Time

To realize the value of ONE YEAR, ask a student who failed a grade.

To realize the value of ONE MONTH, ask a mother who gave birth to a premature baby.

To realize the value of ONE WEEK, ask the editor of a weekly newspaper.

To realize the value of ONE HOUR, ask two lovers who are waiting to meet.

To realize the value of ONE MINUTE, ask a person who missed the plane.

To realize the value of ONE-SECOND, ask a person who just avoided an accident.

To realize the value of ONE MILLISECOND, ask the person who won a silver medal in the Olympics.

To realize the value of ONE NANO-SECOND, ask someone just about to die... who wanted to live little longer.

Time Management

A Human Prerogative

Lower species lead a life without needing a watch or a calender. For all their activities they depend on their inbuilt biological clock. Birds know precisely when to head home before it gets too dark and nocturnal animals know precisely when to reach their den before daybreak.

Pets seem to know when it's time for dinner, go for a walk or a family member to arrive home from work. Sometimes, it appears as if our best animal friends have internal clocks that are precisely synchronized to our home clocks.

Animals simply follow their natural instincts. There is no question of doing any overtime work or shifts. Time management is in fact a prerogative of developed human intelligence. Here also, it depends on the person's consciousness.

A street bum is completely oblivious to the passage of time whereas the president of the country is concerned with every passing minute of his time.

Try To Imagine A Life Without Timekeeping

You probably can't. You know the month, the year, the day of the week. There is a clock on your wall or the dashboard of your car. You have a schedule, a calender, a time for dinner or a movie.

Yet all around you, timekeeping is ignored. Birds are not late. A dog does not check his watch. Deer do not fret over passing birthdays.

Man alone measures time.

Man alone chimes the hour.

And, because of this, man alone suffers a paralyzing fear that no other creature endures.

A fear of time running out."

Reference:

Mitch Albom, The Time Keeper

The "knowledge" of the common man is always in the mode of darkness or ignorance because every living entity in conditional life is born into the mode of ignorance. One who does not develop knowledge through the authorities or scriptural injunctions has knowledge that is limited to the body. He is not concerned about acting in terms of the directions of scripture. For him God is money, and knowledge means the satisfaction of bodily demands. Such knowledge has no connection with the Absolute Truth. It is more or less like the knowledge of the ordinary animals: the knowledge of eating, sleeping, defending and mating. Such knowledge is described here as the product of the mode of darkness.

~ Srila Prabhupada (Bhagavad Gita 18.22)

What Is Time Management

Time management is the act or process of planning and exercising conscious control over the amount of time spent on specific activities, especially to increase effectiveness, efficiency or productivity.

It is a meta-activity with the goal to maximize the overall benefit of a set of other activities within the boundary condition of a limited amount of time.

Time management may be aided by a range of skills, tools, and techniques used to manage time when accomplishing specific tasks, projects, and goals complying with a due date. Initially,

We should not waste our time reading and talking nonsense, but should engage in the study of Srimad-Bhagavatam. Our time is very valuable, and we should not waste it. Chankya Pandita has said: ayusah ksana eko pi na labhyah svarna kotibhih. We may live for a hundred years, but not one moment of these hundred years can be returned, not even if we are prepared to pay millions of dollars. We cannot add a moment, nor can we get a moment back. If time is money, we should just consider how much money we have lost. However, time is even more precious because it cannot be regained. Therefore not a single moment should be lost.

~ Srila Prabhupada (Teaching of Lord Kapila, Vs16)

time management referred to just business or work activities, but eventually the term broadened to include personal activities as well.

A time management system is a designed combination of processes, tools, techniques, and methods. Time management is usually a necessity in any project development as it determines the project completion time and scope.

"Part-time employees are expected to work 24 hours a day. Full-time employees are expected to work 48 hours a day."

The major themes arising from the literature on time management include the following:

Creating an environment conducive to effectiveness

Setting of priorities

Carrying out activity around those priorities

The related process of reduction of time spent on non-priorities

Time management

A Misnomer

L et's face it, time management is really self management. The challenge is not to manage time, but to manage ourselves. No matter how organized we are, there are always only 24 hours in a day. Time doesn't change. All we can actually manage is ourselves and what we do with the time that we have.

Time management might seem like the best way to become time rich, but it rarely helps pull people out of time poverty. People use time management to become more efficient. Time management provides ways to pack more into your schedule and get more done each day. Unfortunately, life's tasks are endless. You might get more done, but you probably won't have any extra free time to do things that are fulfilling to you.

"Time management is a myth. If I had any control over time, I'd still be sixteen years old and weigh 90 pounds!"

Many times these concept of time management fall to deaf ears because these approaches just focus on saving time to earn more or to accomplish more or to simply enhance the enjoyment more. But someone who enjoys 'wasting' time is perfectly in line with these approaches. After all when the goal is to maximize enjoyment, it makes little difference then whether it comes by 'utilizing' time or 'wasting' time,

One person is playing fiddle under a tree in broad daylight when everyone else is busily scurrying about. One person approaches the gentleman,"Why don't you take up a job?" "What do I gain?", asks our friend, dryly. The person replies'"Well! You can make money that way."

"Why or what for should I make money?"

"Money is the basis for our survival and you can invest it in various ways".

"But why should we bother to invest?".

"Well than you make more money by multiplying it."

"Then what happens" asks the fiddler, nonchalantly.

"You can buy a nice house, a big car and a farm in the countryside."

"Then?",

A great Indian scientist, busy in the planmaking business, was suddenly called by invincible eternal time while going to attend a very important meeting of the planning commission, and he had to surrender his life, wife, children, house, land, wealth, etc. During the political upsurge in India and its division into Pakistan and Hindustan, so many rich and influential Indians had to surrender life, property and honor due to the influence of time, and there are hundreds and thousands of examples like that all over the world, all over the universe, which are all effects of the influence of time. Therefore, the conclusion is that there is no powerful living being within the universe who can overcome the influence of time. Many poets have written verses lamenting the influence of time. Many devastations have taken place over the universes due to the influence of time, and no one could check them by any means. Even in our daily life, so many things come and go in which we have no hand, but we have to suffer or tolerate them without remedial measure. That is the result of time.

~ Srila Prabhupada (Srimad Bhagavatam 1.13.20)

"Well...you can retire peacefully and stay in your farm!"
"Then?", asks the fiddler with quizzical looks in his eyes.
"You can peacefully sit under a tree and play a fiddle!"
Snaps our friend, "That I am already doing!"

Time Inventory

Assessing Your Time Expenditures

Have you ever truly looked at where you are spending your time, virtually, minute by minute? This is the first order of business because I am sure you will be surprised. The first step to learning how to manage your time is to see how you are using it now. Once you know how you are spending your time, you can make changes to be more productive. Then you can take your friends, family members and employees on the same journey and end up with an awesome group of efficient people who change other people's lives for the better!

A time inventory is done by taking a small journal, calendar or notebook and writing down everything that you do during the day. This can be done for three or four days but really shows itself to be most effective when you can do it for a week or two, since there

"Hi, good to hear from you.
Yes, I'm just back from that time management seminar.
Sure, I can talk for a couple of seconds.
So, about that meeting tomorr...Oops, time's up. Well, goodbye."

are many things that we only do one time per week.

Begin to track what you spend your time on. Write down everything. If you spend ten minutes on the phone, write it down. If you sleep for eight hours write it down. If you eat lunch for 45 minutes, write it down. If you commute 35 minutes each way, write it down. If you watch television for 3 hours, write it down.

Certainly even one day will begin to reveal some of your patterns. Even a basic day may show that you sleep for eight hours, eat for two and half hours, work for eight hours, drive for one and a half hours, talk on the phone for three hours, and watch television for three and a half hours, among other things of course! What you will begin to realize is that you are spending the right amount of time on some things and it appropriately fits your priorities. Other things you may realize that you are neglecting. And certainly you will see that there are things you are spending an inordinate amount of time on that are opposed to your priorities.

After a few days or so of doing this, sit down and total up your "spending." What does it look like? Where did it all go? Are you happy with how you spent it? These things will become clear, because if you track it moment by moment, the numbers will not lie.

Here's what's important to understand… time is more valuable than money. You can get more money, but you can't get more time. Once it's spent, it's gone. Assessing our time expenditures is the first step, because it will show us that often our memory of how we spent our time can be a little "foggy." It's powerful when we understand, grasp and apply the principle of wisely budgeting our time because we can help ourselves first and then we can help others.

Reference:

Donna Krech, Success with Substance, 2013

Every Moment Counts

Every Second Matters

Imagine if there were a bank that credits your account each morning with $86,400, and carries over no balance from day to day. Every evening it deletes whatever part of the balance you failed to use during the day.

What would you do? Draw out all of it, of course.

Each of us has such a bank. It's name is Time.

Every morning, it credits us with 86,400 seconds. Every night it writes off, as lost, whatever of this we have failed to invest to good purpose. It carries over no balance. It allows no overdraft.

Life is so valuable that we cannot waste even a second without any profit. That is the aim of life. The materialist persons, especially in country like yours, they calculate... I do not know. When I was in India I heard it that if you go to see an important businessman, his secretary, while talking with that man, the secretary gives you a card that "This Mr. such and such cannot spare more than two minutes." Is it a fact? Anyway, we should not waste our time, either you act materially or spiritually.

~ Srila Prabhupada (Lecture, Srimad Bhagavatam 7.6.6, New Vrindaban, June 22, 1976)

Doing The Right Thing

At The Right Time

Many people associate successful people with good time management. Much of that success is attributed to the statement "doing the right thing, at the right time". People often say that successful people are blessed with money and resources, yet they did not all start out like this. While most successful business people have personal assistants and secretaries, the reason that they are successful is derived precisely from the above statement. They are doing the right thing at the right time. They have clarity on how to prioritise and focus on the important tasks. Many of these successful people are highly disciplined and organised or they surround themselves with people who are. They know the basic principles of time management and how to succeed.

Chankya, the great philosopher says, "Three things should be taken care of immediately: Fire, disease and debt." A fire which can be extinguished now with a cup of water might not come under control of ten fire engines later on.

References:
William Yellowwood

Do It All Now

The Immediate Gratification Mentality

Our culture teaches us that if something is good we should seek to enjoy it immediately. So we microwave our food, instead of cooking the traditional way, e-mail our letters instead of sending by the postal service, and express mail our packages.

We do our best to escape the confines of time by accelerating our schedules, speeding up our pace, and doing whatever it takes to beat the clock. How did you respond the last time you had to wait in line for something? Did you patiently wait your turn, or did you tap your toe and try to rush the experience?

Our "do it all now" mentality has tremendously affected the timing of everything we do in life. Kids involve themselves in dating and even sexual relationships at an increasingly young age. As young people rush prematurely into these adult activities, most of their elders do little to correct them. After all what can adults say when they live by the same "grab it all now" attitude?

Why do we insist on living this way? We adopt the immediate gratification mentality because we've lost sight of the natural principle of seasons. Just as spring's role is different from that of fall, so each of the seasons of our lives has a different emphasis, focus and beauty. One is not better than the other; each season yields its own unique treasures. We cannot skip ahead to experience the riches of another life season any more than a farmer can rush the spring. Each season builds on the one before it.

God has many wonderful experiences He wants to give to us, but He also assigns these particular experiences to particular seasons of our lives. In our humaneness, we often make the mistake of taking a good thing out of its appropriate season to enjoy it when we want it. Like a fruit picked green or a flower

"I have metal fillings in my teeth. My refrigerator magnets keep pulling me into the kitchen. That's why I can't lose weight!"

plucked before it blossoms, our attempts to rush God's timing can spoil the beauty of His plan for our lives.

Just because something is good doesn't mean we should pursue it right now. We have to remember that the right thing at the wrong time is the wrong thing.

Reference:

I Kissed Dating Goodbye: A New Attitude Toward Relationships and Romance Paperback, Joshua Harris

---

They are two things. Preya means which I like immediately, very nice. And sreya means ultimate goal. They are two things. Just like a child wants to play all day. That is childish nature. That is preya. And sreya means he must take education so that in future his life will be settled up. That is sreya. So Arjuna is asking not preya. He's asking instruction from Krsna for the purpose of confirming his sreya. Preya means immediately he was thinking: "I shall be happy by not fighting, not by killing my kinsmen." That, he was, like a child, he was thinking. But when he came to his consciousness... Not actually consciousness, because he's intelligent. He's asking for sreya. Yac chreyah syat. "What is the, actually, my ultimate goal of life?" ~ Srila Prabhupada (Bhagavad-gita 2.7 -- London, August 7, 1973)

Doing The Right Thing

At The Wrong Time

Doing the right thing at the wrong time is still the wrong thing. In Shakespeare's play Julius Caesar, Brutus was the one who uttered the words: "There is a tide in the affairs of men, which taken at the flood, leads on to fortune." Timing is mightily important and all happenings in our life is heavily dependent on timing for their success.

In the Old Testament book Ecclesiastes, traditionally ascribed to Solomon (970–928 BC), time was traditionally regarded as a medium for the passage of predestined events. (Another word, zman, was current as meaning time fit for an event, and is used as the modern Arabic, Persian, and Hebrew equivalent to the English word "time".)

There is an appointed time (zman) for everything. And there is a time ('êth) for every event under heaven–

A time ('êth) to give birth, and a time to die; A time to plant, and a time to uproot what is planted.

A time to kill, and a time to heal; A time to tear down, and a time to build up.

A time to weep, and a time to laugh; A time to mourn, and a time to dance.

A time to throw stones, and a time to gather stones; A time to embrace, and a time to shun embracing.

A time to search, and a time to give up as lost; A time to keep, and a time to throw away.

A time to tear apart, and a time to sew together; A time to be silent, and a time to speak.

A time to love, and a time to hate; A time for war, and a time for peace. – Ecclesiastes 3:1–8

Everything should be done at the proper time. One should rise by four o'clock in the morning and utilize the auspicious brahma-muhūrta to advance in Krsna consciousness. Similarly, one should avoid the sinful influence of hours such as midnight when ghosts and demons are encouraged to become active. Concerning work, one should execute one's prescribed duties, follow the regulative principles of spiritual life and utilize all of one's energy for pious purposes. Time should not be wasted in frivolous or materialistic activities, of which there are now literally millions in modern society.

~ Srila Prabhupada (Srimad Bhagavatam 11.13.6)

Better Never

Than Late

There are many things in life that would have been better left undone than done late. English playwright, William Shakespeare, once said better three hours too soon than a minute late.' In some aspect or the other, we are already late in life. Life's tragedy is that 'we get old too soon and wise too late.'

Douglas Adams portrays chronic lateness when he says, "I love deadlines. I love the whooshing noise they make as they go by." Those who are habitually late, miss the bus in life. There are couple of stories that elaborate on this point.

The Priest And The Politician

After twenty-five years in the same parish, Father O'Shaunessey was saying his farewells at his retirement dinner. An eminent member of the congregation - a leading politician - had been asked to make a presentation and a short speech, but was late arriving.

So the priest took it upon himself to fill the time, and stood up to the microphone:

"I remember the first confession I heard here twenty-five years ago and it worried me as to what sort of place I'd come to... That first confession remains the worst I've ever heard. The chap confessed that he'd stolen a TV set from a neighbour and lied to the police when questioned, successfully blaming it on a local scallywag. He said that he'd stolen money from his parents and from his employer; that he'd had affairs with several of his friends' wives; that he'd taken hard drugs, and had slept with his sister and given her VD. You can imagine what I thought... However I'm pleased to say that as the days passed I soon realised that this sad fellow was a frightful exception and that this parish was indeed a wonderful place full of kind and decent people..."

At this point the politician arrived and apologised for being late, and keen to take the stage, he immediately stepped up to the microphone and pulled his speech from his pocket:

"Sorry I'm late dear... have you been waiting long?"

"I'll always remember when Father O'Shaunessey first came to our parish," said the politician, "In fact, I'm pretty certain that I was the first person in the parish that he heard in confession..."

Late May Be As Good As Never

There was lazy boy and he always used to postpone things. One day, he came to know that he had won the first prize in a singing

It is important to take to this consciousness immediately, because we do not know how much time is left before death. When your time in this body expires, no one can stop your death. The arrangement of material nature is so strong. You cannot say, "Let me remain." Actually, people sometimes request like that. When I was in Allahabad, an old friend who was very rich was dying. At that time he begged the doctor, "Can't you give me at least four more years to live? I have some plans which I could not finish." "Oh, no, sir. Not four years, not even four minutes. You have to go immediately." This is the law. So before that moment comes, one should be very careful to become realized in Krsna consciousness.

~ Srila Prabhuapda (God and The Law of Karma)

49

competition that was held the previous month. He was asked to collect the prize the same day.

He didn't care and went to collect the prize the next day. But the prize had become useless for him, as it was a ticket to a circus show, which was held the previous day.

Sometimes Time Moves Quickly

Sometimes It Seems To Slow Down

Sometimes time moves quickly, and in some situations time seems to slow down. All of this ultimately has a neural representation.

Keeping track of time is one of the brain's most important tasks. As the brain processes the flood of sights and sounds it encounters, it must also remember when each event occurred. But how does that happen? How does your brain recall that you brushed your teeth before you took a shower, and not the other way around?

For decades, neuroscientists have theorized that the brain "time stamps" events as they happen, allowing us to keep track of where we are in time and when past events occurred. However, they couldn't find any evidence that such time stamps really existed -- until now.

In bed, it's 6:00am.
You close your eyes for 5 minutes, it's 7:45.

At work, it's 1:30.
You close your eyes for 5 minutes, it's: 1:31.

An MIT team led by Institute Professor Ann Graybiel has found groups of neurons in the primate brain that code time with extreme precision. "All you do is time stamp everything, and then recalling events is easy: you go back and look through your time stamps until you see which ones are correlated with the event," she says.

That kind of precise timing control is critical for everyday tasks such as driving a car or playing the piano, as well as keeping track of past events. The discovery was reported in the proceedings of the National Academy of Sciences.

Construction Of Time

The research team trained two macaque monkeys to perform a simple eye-movement task. After receiving the "go" signal, the monkeys were free to perform the task at their own speed. The researchers found neurons that consistently fired at specific times - 100 milliseconds, 110 milliseconds, 150 milliseconds and so on - after the "go" signal.

"Soon enough we realized we had cells keeping time, which everyone has wanted to find, but nobody has found them before," says Graybiel, who is also an investigator in MIT's McGovern Institute for Brain Research. The neurons are located in the prefrontal cortex and the striatum, both of which play important roles in learning, movement and thought control.

The new work is an elegant demonstration of how the brain represents time, says Peter Strick, professor of neurobiology at the University of Pittsburgh, who was not involved in the research. "We have sensory receptors for light, sound, touch, hot and cold, and smell, but we don't have sensory receptors for time. This is a sense constructed by the brain," he says.

The Personality of Godhead said: As a mass of clouds does not know the powerful influence of the wind, a person engaged in material consciousness does not know the powerful strength of the time factor, by which he is being carried.
~ Srila Prabhupada (Srimad Bhagavatam 3.30.1)

Reference:

Jin DZ, Fujii N, Graybiel AM. Neural representation of time in corticobasal ganglia circuits. Proceedings of the National Academy of Sciences, Week of Oct. 19 2009 Massachusetts Institute of Technology

We Don't Control Time

But We Can Control Our Perception

Perceived Time vs. Clock Time

According to Steve Taylor, clock time may be about minutes and hours but perceived time is down to how we experience it and it differs from person to person. Perceived time is a subjective perception of time in which things are perceived as passing by faster or slower than the normal perception of time.

To a bystander watching a life-threatening situation such as an accident, time is moving at a normal speed. However, to the individual in the accident, time seems to have slowed down. As a result, the individual in the accident may be able to think faster and act faster during these events. During high-stress situations like this, the brain receives massive amounts of data to process which alters the brain's perception of time. Therefore, during an accident a person can react quickly and make a decision in a very short period of time.

Einstein is reported to have said something like 'When a man sits with a pretty girl for an hour, it seems like a minute. But let

Insurmountable, eternal time imperceptibly overcomes those who are too much attached to worldy affairs and are always engrossed in their thought.

~ Srila Prabhupada (Srimad Bhagavatam 1.13.17)

him sit on a hot stove for a minute and it's longer than any hour. That's relativity.'

If you find yourself having a job, you will notice that some days go by fast - and some days crawl by really slowly. The slow days are when you have checked in with the outer world many times, as will often happen when the work you are doing isn't very engaging to your brain. On the other hand, even a stressful day can go by really quickly if you are totally focused on your task. If you have something difficult and absorbing to do, you will tend to concentrate on it to the exclusion of distracting sensory input.

Steve Taylor narrates a childhood experience on time perception.

I'm six years old, in the car with my parents and brother, travelling back from our annual two week holiday in Conwy, North Wales. It's dark and the journey seems to take forever. I lie in the back seat, watching the orange streetlights and the houses pass by, and wonder if we're ever going to get home.

"Every minute here feels like an hour. Every hour feels like a day. Every day feels like a week. I don't think a time management seminar can fix that."

"Are we nearly there yet?" I ask my father.

"Don't be silly," he says. "We only set off half an hour ago."

My mum plays a few games with us to make the time pass faster. We listen to the radio for a while. Then I fall asleep. When I wake

The Personality of Godhead said: As a mass of clouds does not know the powerful influence of the wind, a person engaged in material consciousness does not know the powerful strength of the time factor, by which he is being carried.

~ Srila Prabhupada (Srimad Bhagavatam 3.30.1)

up it seems like I've been in the car for an eternity and I can't believe we're still not home.

The journey from Conwy to Manchester took two hours when I was a child and still takes roughly two hours now (although slightly less due to improvements in roads). I made the journey again a few years ago and couldn't believe how short it seemed now, from my adult perspective. Those two hours - which seemed like an eternity when I was 6 - were nothing. My girlfriend was driving, and we chatted, listened to tapes, watched the Welsh countryside give way to the urban sprawl of north-west England, and we were back in Manchester almost before we knew it. It was a little frightening - what had happened to all the time that two hours contained when I was six years old?

This story appears to fit with most people's experience. Most of us feel that time moved very slowly when we were children and is gradually speeding up as we grow older.

Reference:
Out of the Darkness, The science of post-traumatic growth, Steve Taylor, July 2011

'There's Not Enough Time'

A Subjective Perception

The catch-phrase "there's not enough time" is probably very familiar to people working on various projects. The specter of the passing hours always looms over their heads, even if, in reality, they have more than sufficient time to complete their task. And this is where a new scientific study comes in. Experts say that the perception people get of time is paramount in determining the quality of their work. In other words, if individuals feel like they have enough time – even though they don't – they are more likely to perform better under stress.

"Research has shown that it's not necessarily the time pressure, but it's the perception of that time pressure that affects you. If you feel you don't have enough time to do something, it's going to affect you," Case Western Reserve University psychology doctoral student Michael DeDonno explains. He has been the leader of the current study, published in the December issue of the journal Judgment and Decision Making, which has examined the cases of 163 test subjects who have taken part in a game called the Iowa Gambling Task (IGT), popular among psychologists.

In this game, participants are told they have to fulfill a task, and are then separated into two groups. One group is informed that it has very little time to complete the assignment, while the other is communicated that it has sufficient time to execute all the demands of the exercise. In reality, both groups are given the same time-frame to accomplish their objectives. The researchers have noted that the people in the group that was told it had not much time were far more likely to make mistakes and work in a sloppier manner than those in the control group.

"If I told you that you didn't have enough time, your performance was low regardless if you had ample time or not. If you were told you had enough time, in both scenarios, they out performed those who were told they didn't,"

DeDonno adds. "Decision-making can be emotion-based, keep your emotions in check. Have confidence in the amount of time you do have to do things. Try to focus on the task and not the time. We don't control time, but we can control our perception. It's amazing what you can do with a limited amount of time. Time is relevant but just have the confidence with the time you're given. I tell my students 'Do the best you can in the time allotted. When it ends, it ends.'"

> *Eternal time is never lost .... It continues, but it has no ability to control the Supreme Personality of Godhead because the Lord is the controller of time. In the spiritual world there is undoubtedly time, but it has no control over activities. Time is unlimited, and the spiritual world is also unlimited, since everything there exists on the absolute plane.*
> *~ Srila Prabhupada (Srimad Bhagavatam 3.11.38)*

Reference:

Perceived time pressure and the Iowa Gambling Task, Michael A. DeDonno and Heath A. Demaree

Department of Psychology, Case Western Reserve University

Judgment and Decision Making, Vol. 3, No. 8, December 2008, pp. 636–640

The Older You Get

The Faster Time Seems To Go

Persons in every age group wonder why time seems to move so much faster than it did in their pasts. It seems as if there is never enough time to get everything done and that the situation only gets worse. Many explanations have been offered for this.

According to Steve Taylor, we usually become conscious of this speeding up around our late twenties, when most of us have 'settled down.' We have steady jobs and marriages and homes and our lives become ordered into routines - the daily routine of working, coming home, having dinner and watching TV; the weekly routine of (for example) going to the gym on Monday night, going to the whatever on Friday night etc.; and the yearly routine of birthdays, bank holidays and two weeks' holiday in the summer. After a few years we start to realise that the time it takes us to run through these

> *When as a child I laughed and wept, time crept. When as a youth I waxed more bold, time strolled. When I became a full-grown man, time RAN. When older still I daily grew, time FLEW. Soon I shall find, in passing on, time gone.*
> *~ Twells, Henry*

routines seems to be decreasing, as if we're on a turntable which is picking up speed with every rotation.

This speeding up is probably responsible for the phenomenon which psychologists call 'forward telescoping': our tendency to think that past events have happened more recently than they actually have. Marriages, deaths, the birth of children - when we look back at these and other significant events, we're often surprised that they happened so long ago, shocked to find that it's already four years since a friend died when we thought it was only a couple of years, or that a niece or nephew is already ten years old when it only seems like three or four years since they were born.

According to Philip Yaffe, an author and journalist, it's really quite simple. It all has to do with "anticipation" and "retrospection".

Whatever the nature of our individual lives, we all anticipate things important to us. Then after they happen, we look back at them. For example, most school children look forward to the long summer vacation, which always seems to be an eternity away. Finally,

Time is figuratively described here as Chandavega. Since time and tide wait for no man, time is herein called Chandavega, which means "very swiftly passing away." As time passes, it is calculated in terms of years. One year contains 360 days, and the soldiers of Chandavega herein mentioned represent these days. Time passes swiftly; Chandavega's powerful soldiers of Gandharvaloka very swiftly carry away all the days of our life. As the sun rises and sets, it snatches away the balance of our life-span. Thus as each day passes, each one of us loses some of life's duration. It is therefore said that the duration of one's life cannot be saved. But if one is engaged in devotional service, his time cannot be taken away by the sun.

~ Srila Prabhupada (Srimad Bhagavatam 4.27.13)

it arrives. Then, almost before they blink an eye, it's over and they are back in school again.

Progressing from primary school to secondary school is another excruciating anticipation for a youngster, especially if the move is perceived as being an important step away from childhood into adulthood.

And so it goes. When anticipated, each new significant event seems to be excruciatingly far away. However, after the event, we regularly look back and exclaim. "Did it really happen that long ago?"

Our first love, our first heartbreak, driving a car, landing a job, marriage, etc. When we look forward, all these milestones seem impossibly far in the future. However once achieved, how quickly they recede into the past.

The older we get, the more milestones we have to look back on. So the farther and faster they appear to recede. So if sometimes the clock may seem to have stopped, the calendar always continues racing ahead.

Reference:

Why Does Time Go Faster As We Get Older?

October 2008, By Philip Yaffe

Out of the Darkness, The science of post-traumatic growth, Steve Taylor, July 2011

Life

Where Do All Our Days Go?

Nothing is swifter than our years and the longest day soon comes to an end. Time is very swiftly passing away. The clock is running away. Try catch hold of whatever you can.

Ever wonder what happens to life? How years pass away like moments, before we even have time to catch a breath.

Following is an average usage of time in the life of an ordinary human being. This goes to show that unless we are very conscious of time and manage it wisely, we will have no time for higher pursuits in life.

<u>Average Usage Of Time</u>

A - Sleeping (average 8 hrs)	33%
B - Eating, Bathing & Other Bodily Activities(Average 2 hrs)	8%
C - Childhood Innocense	5%
D - Youthful Playhood	5%
E - Earning Livelihood	25%
F - Old Age Invalidity	10%
G - Studies, Commuting, Recreation, etc.	14%
Total	100%

There is another estimate on how we spend our lifetime.

7 Time Consuming Things An Average Person Spends On In A Lifetime

Have you ever wondered how much time you spend on certain activities in a lifetime? When our day-to-day activities are summed up into a lifetime, it can be frightening to see how much of our lives goes into these tasks. We've put together seven time consuming things an average person spends on in their lifetime.

1. Sleeping

A good night's sleep is vital for every human being to survive. Given that an average a person sleeps for 8 hours in a day, that means that an average person will sleep for 229,961 hours in their lifetime or basically one third of their life. That's precious time which could have been spent watching Die Hard 105,325 times.

I Expected It

But Not So Soon

2. Eating

Eating is a necessary part of life that we must do in order to survive. A study done in the US said that an average American spends 67 minutes per day eating and drinking beverages. Summed up together, the average person spends a staggering 32,098 hours (almost 4 years) eating and drinking beverages in their lifetime.

3. Driving

Cruising down the street on a warm sunny day can be a great joy, but driving can also be kind of a drag. According to a study done by the Harvard Health Watch, an average American spends 101

Although one has a maximum of one hundred years of life, by sleeping one loses fifty years. Eating, sleeping, sex life and fear are the four bodily necessities, but to utilize the full duration of life a person desiring to advance in spiritual consciousness must reduce these activities. That will give him an opportunity to fully use his lifetime.

~ Srila Prabhupada (SB 7.6.6)

minutes per day driving. That means that in a lifetime, an average person spends a whopping 37,935 hours driving a car (assuming that s/he starts driving at 17 and drives until 78.7 years old). In that time, average person will drive around 798,000 miles (1,284,256 kilometers), which is approximately the distance it takes to drive to the moon more than three times! That is almost 4.5 years of life gone in driving.

4. Working

Work is a big part of our life and our biggest source of income, but how much time do we actually spend working? Let's say that average person works 40 hours a week, from the age of 20-65 and gets two weeks of vacation every year. In that time, average Person will have worked a total of 90,360 hours of his life working for the man. That is almost 11 years of his life gone in the job.

5. Surfing The Internet

In the past decade, the impact of the Internet has exploded, becoming an integral part of our everyday lives. We work, shop, socialize, play games, educate, read news, and do so many other things online. A study done in 2010 tells us that an average American spends 32 hours per month online. That totals 28,300 hours (3.5 years) in a lifetime, and this number may increase in the future with smart devices becoming more commonly used and allowing easier access to the Internet.

6. Watching TV

Most of us love watching TV as a leisure activity. According to the US Bureau of Labor Statistics the average American watched TV for 2.8 hours per day, accounting, on average, for around half of their leisure time. That means an average person will watch TV for 80,486 hours. That means over 9 years of human life gone idling in front of the idiot box.

7. Cleaning

Most of us don't like to clean very much but unfortunately it's something that most of us have to do. According to this article, women will spend 12,896 hours in their lifetime cleaning the home, which is almost one-and-a-half year of their lives. It may not be a huge surprise that men spend less time cleaning in their lifetime as compared to women. Men spend around half of that — or 6,448 hours in their lifetime cleaning.

The calculation were based on the life expectancy that average person will live to be 78.7 years old according to life expectancy at birth for the U.S. population in 2011

When calculating how much time is spent driving we assumed that an average Person would drive from the age of 17 till his death.

When calculating time spent online we estimated that a person would start using the internet at the age of 5.

Track Your Life - By Tracking Your Time

William Penn once said "Time is what we want most, but what we use worst."We may not always be able to control how we spend our time, but we can try to make the most of it.

The best way to gain awareness — the first step towards change — is to find an objective system of measurement that cuts through the power of human rationalization. After all, perception and reality are often two different things. When you track your time, you get a healthy dose of the unfettered truth. Then you can start spending time on what's most important.

For most of us, time tracking is more about making every hour count than it is about counting every hour. That is, time tracking is not just about awareness: it's about change. Perhaps this is the crux of why time tracking means getting things done: hours don't lie. When you realize how you spend your time, it makes clear where your priorities are — or ought to be — and it shows you how you might make your time better match your priorities.

Therefore unless time is very carefully managed, there is very little scope for higher pursuits in life and we always remain infected with the disease known as "no time".

There is another interesting survey published in Daily Mirror which sheds further light on the subject.

Fascinating Facts About How We Spend The Days Of Our Lives

By Mirror.co.uk, Aug 06

136 days women spend getting ready

Applying make-up, having a shower and dressing up for a night out uses up a total of 3,276 hours in a girl's lifetime, says a study by body wash firm Skinbliss.

99,117hrs at work

The average British bloke spends all this time grafting at work, according to recent Government statistics. That"s the equivalent of 11 and a half years of solid slog.

23,214hrs washing clothes

It's a dirty job - and now Newstrategist research shows we spend three years of our lives washing our smalls.

115 days laughing

We spend six minutes a day laughing, but we're more miserable than we used to be - in the 50s we spent three times as long having a chuckle, says an Ocean Village poll.

2,170hrs sunbathing.

We spend the equivalent of 13 weeks of our lives on a beach, trying to top up our tans, according to a TripAdvisor survey. And still we're left with white bits!

653hrs waiting for trains

Hanging around on platforms waiting for your train, or queuing at bus stops, takes up 27 days - although it often feels much longer than that.

160days on fag breaks

Smokers really are shortening their lives - by wasting more than five months on average popping out for a crafty ciggy, says the Benenden Healthcare Society.

7 years of insomnia

Canadian health experts have worked out that this is how long we spend lying awake at night waiting for sleep.

6 months queuing

No wonder it seems to take ages getting to the front of a queue. We spend nearly three days waiting in them over a year, and six months over a lifetime, according to a survey by auction site madbid. com.

20wks on hold during a call

That's 60 hours a year listening to music while waiting to speak to a human in a call centre.

4yrs on the phone at work

And this doesn't include calls at home for office workers, according to

Working Lives researchers at London Metropolitan University.

658hrs getting romantic

This is the account of one hundred years of life. Although in this age a lifetime of one hundred years is generally not possible, even if one has one hundred years, the calculation is that fifty years are wasted in sleeping, twenty years in childhood and boyhood, and twenty years in invalidity (jara-vyadhi). This leaves only a few more years, but because of too much attachment to household life, those years are also spent with no purpose, without God consciousness. Therefore, one should be trained to be a perfect brahmachari in the beginning of life and then to be perfect in sense control, following the regulative principles, if one becomes a householder. From household life one is ordered to accept vanaprastha life and go to the forest and then accept sannyāsa. That is the perfection of life. From the very beginning of life, those who are ajitendriya, who cannot control their senses, are educated only for sense gratification, as we have seen in the Western countries. Thus the entire duration of a life of even one hundred years is wasted and misused, and at the time of death one transmigrates to another body, which may not be human. At the end of one hundred years, one who has not acted as a human being in a life of tapasya (austerity and penance) must certainly be embodied again in a body like those of cats, dogs and hogs. Therefore this life of lusty desires and sense gratification is extremely risky.

~ Srila Prabhupada (Srimad Bhagavtam 7.6.8)

British couples will snuggle up and watch the sunset or enjoy a cosy drink on holiday for the equivalent of almost a month during their lifetime, according to TripAdvisor.

3,000hrs shaving

Mr Average might bristle to discover just how much time he will waste shaving - 3,000 hours in a lifetime, reckons a Readers' Digest survey.

366 days off sick

The average Brit spends a year of their working life off sick, says the Confederation of British Industry.

11 years in front of the TV

If you are stuck in front of the goggle box for the average of four hours a day that adds up to 11 years. And in all that time you still you won't find much worth watching.

5months complaining

We spend eight minutes every day moaning about bad service, according to a poll by Hilary Blinds.

38,003hrs eating

You can't rush a full English fry-up, a light lunch, a hearty dinner or even a few snacks. No wonder eating consumes so much of our lives.

5yrs on the net

Log on for the average of 11 hours and 20 minutes a month and, says Nielsen, over a lifetime that is 10,000 hours spent surfing the net!

46,800hrs of housework

The average married woman spends five-and-a-half years dusting, hoovering and keeping the house spic and span.

26yrs sleeping

Over a lifetime you'll spend 227,468 hours tucked up in bed and sound asleep, says the Organisation for Economic Co-operation and Development.

46 days men spend getting ready

Preparing for a lads' night out can't be rushed - and men spend 1,092 hours at it, according to Skinbliss.

References:

http://www.thefreelibrary.com

How+much+time+do+Americans+spend+eating%3F-a0190462486 http://www lifeinthefastlane.ca/life-and-time-spent-by-the-average-person-blow/offbeat-news

http://www.cdc.gov/nchs/fastats/lifexpec.htm

http://www.cdc.gov/nchs/fastats/deaths.htm

http://www.cdc.gov/nchs/data/databriefs/db115.htm

http://www.space.com/18145-how-far-is-the-moon.html

http://www.revolutionhealth.com/blogs/drscherger/men-moderate-exercis-3815

http://www.bls.gov/news.release/atus.nr0.htm

http://www.comscoredatamine.com/2011/01/average-time-spent-online-per-u-s-visitor-in-2010/

http://www.mirror.co.uk/news/uk-news/fascinating-facts-about-how-we-spend-the-days-410973#ixzz2y9TyWN9H

Divisions Of Time

For applying Techniques of Time Mangement

Time can be divided into three aspects for applying techniques of managing it:

(a) Biological: Pertaining to bodily functions.

(b) Social: Pertaining to self, family and society.

(c) Professional: Pertaining to professional activities/time spent at work.

It is essential to maintain equilibrium between these three aspects. Any imbalance may prove to be detrimental to one's physical and mental health and can adversely affect the individual in the long run.

It is essential, therefore, to allocate one's time in balanced manner to the extent feasible to all these three aspects.

Biological Time

Adopt the golden mean of moderation among:

(i) Sleep

(ii) Food

(iii) Ablutions / Calls of nature

(iv) Recreation

(v) Physical Exercise

It is advantageous to establish regularity for all the above activities.

Social Time

It is desirable to give time to yourself, your family and for society and the general guide lines are:

(i) Self-development/self time:

At least one hour per day should be kept for oneself for thinking, introspection, reading and other hobbies.

(ii) Family time:

Strong family ties and a peaceful domestic life are the foundations of success in both personal and professional life. One must spend some time with one's family everyday and to co-ordinate activities with family members.

(iii) Social time:

In order to live in society, one has to attend various social events, like weddings, religious

GLASBERGEN

"Time management is a great concept, but who has time for it?!"

functions etc., where one is not the master of one's own time. Social obligations may entail a substantial portion of time.

It is advised that one observe the eternal time factor, which is the cause of the material body's appearance and disappearance, and that one observe the living entity's entanglement in this time factor.

~ Srila Prabhupada (Srimad Bhagavatam 7.13.6)

Professional Time

In this aspect, if one is working, one does not really have a choice as working hours are generally fixed. The aim here is to optimally utilise the available time for maximum output/productivity and self-satisfaction.

It is, therefore, essential to plan one's work and that of the subordinates in an efficient manner and also identify 'time wasters' and make efforts to eliminate/reduce them. Examples of time wasters are:

(i) Infructuous meetings
(ii) Poor communication
(iii) Unwanted visitors
(iv) Disorganised work etc.

So this is going on under the influence of kala. So people should be enlightened that "Don't remain asleep." Uttisthata jagrata prapya varän nibodhata. "Now you are civilized human being. You can read and write. You can understand." So jägrata: "Now get up, be awakened. Study this Vedic literature, especially the essence of Vedic literature, Srimad-Bhägavatam."
~ *Srila Prabhupada (Lecture, Srimad-Bhägavatam 3.26.17 -- Bombay, December 26, 1974)*

You Can't Catch One Hog

When You're Chasing Two

Human multitasking is the apparent performance by an individual of handling more than one task at the same time. You're on the phone with a supplier, while quietly typing up notes about your previous phone call.

As soon as you hang up, a colleague sends you an instant message, which you read over while dialing your manager's extension number.

Then, during your phone conversation with her, you start updating your week's to-do-list.

To boost our productivity, many of us multitask like this to some degree. And, in a world where the pace of life is often frantic, people who can multitask are typically seen as efficient and effective. After all, don't we get more done when we do more than one thing at a time?

Actually, multitasking doesn't make us as productive as we think. What's more, it's likely that the quality of our work is worse when we multitask. In fact, it could actually be costing us time instead of creating it.

The term is derived from computer multitasking. The term "multitasking" originated in the computer engineering industry. It refers to the ability of a microprocessor to apparently process several tasks simultaneously.

In this article we'll examine the issues associated with multitasking, and look at why we shouldn't do it. We'll also look at some suggestions to help you get out of the multitasking habit.

Is Multitasking Costing You Time?

Multitasking and the Myth of Productivity

Many people have studied multitasking over the last decade, and most of them have come to the same conclusion: Multitasking doesn't make us more productive!

Several studies have found that multitasking can actually result in us wasting around 20-40 percent of our time, depending on what we're trying to do.

The simple reason that multitasking doesn't work is because we can't actually focus on more than one task at a time. But we think we can – so we multitask to try and get more done.

Imagine trying to talk to someone and write an email at the same time. Both of these tasks involve communication. You can't speak to someone and write a really clear and focused email at the same time. The tasks are too conflicting – your mind gets overloaded as you try to switch between the two tasks.

Now think about listening to someone as you try to write an email. These two tasks are a bit easier to do together because they involve different skills. But your attention to the person will fade

> *When you are standing on two boats you'll never be satisfied. It is very dangerous position, you know? Two boats, on the river, and if you put one leg here, one leg here, it is always troublesome. Either you give up this or give up that. Then your position will be safe.*
> *~ Srila Prabhupada (Morning Walk -- April 7, 1975, Mayapur)*

in and out as you're writing. You simply can't fully focus on both things at once.

The biggest problem with multitasking is that it can lower the quality of our work – we try to do two things or more things at once, and the result is that we do everything less well than if we focused properly on each task in turn.

When we switch tasks, our minds must reorient to cope with the new information. If we do this rapidly, like when we're multitasking, we simply can't devote our full concentration and focus to every switch. So the quality of our work suffers. The more complex or technical the tasks we're switching between, the bigger the drop in quality is likely to be. For instance, it would be almost impossible to write a good-quality presentation while having an emotionally charged conversation with a co-worker!

Another major downside to multitasking is the effect it has on our stress levels. Dealing with multiple things at once makes us feel overwhelmed, drained and frazzled.

On the other hand, think of how satisfied you feel when you devote your full attention to one task. You're able to focus, and you'll probably finish it feeling as if you've not only completed something, but done it well. This is called being in flow , and it's a skill that can be developed with some practice.

Psychiatrist Edward M. Hallowell has gone so far as to describe multitasking as a "mythical activity in which people believe they can perform two or more tasks simultaneously as effectively as one."

Others have researched multitasking in specific domains, such as learning. Mayer and Moreno have studied the phenomenon of cognitive load in multimedia learning extensively and have concluded that it is difficult, and possibly impossible to learn new information while engaging in multitasking.

Junco and Cotten examined how multitasking affects academic success and found that students who engaged in more multitasking reported more problems with their academic work. A more recent study on the effects of multitasking on academic performance found that using Facebook and text messaging while studying were negatively related to student grades.

Spotting the Multitasking Tendency

It can be hard to identify when you're multitasking. But there are a few key indicators you can look for:

• If you have several pages or tabs open on your computer, then you're probably multitasking. The same goes for your desk – if you have several file folders or papers out that you're working on, you might well be multitasking.

"My dad is a natural at multitasking. He can goof up, screw up, and mess up all at the same time."

• Multitasking is more likely when you're working on a project or task you're not excited about. For instance, creating a spreadsheet analysis might be an unwelcome task, so you might frequently check your email or do some research on a new assignment in order to lessen the pain of the current task.

• Frequent interruptions can also cause you to multitask. For instance, you might be writing your department's budget when a colleague comes into your office with a question for you. You then carry on trying to tinker with the budget as you answer their question.

The Brain's Role

When people attempt to complete many tasks at one time, "or [alternate] rapidly between them, errors go way up and it takes far longer—often double the time or more—to get the jobs done than if they were done sequentially," states Meyer. This is largely because "the brain is compelled to restart and refocus".

According to a study done by Jordan Grafman, "Focusing on multiple dissimilar tasks at once forces the brain to process all activity in its anterior. Though the brain is complex and can perform a myriad of tasks, it cannot multitask well."

Another study by René Marois, a psychologist, when asked to perform several tasks at once, the brain must then decide which activity is most important, thereby taking more time.

People have a limited ability to retain information, which worsens when the amount of information increases. Brains are only capable of storing a limited amount of information in their short term memories.

Role of Technology

Rapidly increasing technology fosters multitasking because it promotes multiple sources of input at a given time. Instead of exchanging old equipment like TV, print, and music, for new equipment such as  computers, the Internet, and video games, children and teens combine forms of media and continually increase sources of input. According to studies by the Kaiser Family Foundation, in 1999 only 16 percent of time spent using media such as internet, television, video games, telephones, text-messaging, or e-mail was combined. In 2005, 26 percent of the time this media was used together. This increase in simultaneous media usage decreases the amount of attention paid to each device. As technology provides more distractions, attention is spread among tasks more thinly.

Hazards

A prevalent example of this inattention to detail due to multitasking is apparent when people talk on cell phones while driving. One study found that having an accident is four times more likely when using a cell phone while driving.

Another study compared reaction times for experienced drivers during a number of tasks, and found that the subjects reacted more slowly to brake lights and stop signs during phone conversations than during other simultaneous tasks.

When talking, people must withdraw their attention from the road in order to formulate responses. Because the brain cannot focus on two sources of input at one time, driving and listening or talking, constantly changing input provided by cell phones distracts the brain and increases the likelihood of accidents.

Gender Differences

Although the idea that women are better multitaskers than men has been popular in the media as well in conventional thought, there is very little data available to support claims of a real gender difference. Most studies that do show any gender differences tend to find that the differences are small and inconsistent.

A study by psychologist Keith Laws was widely reported in the press to have provided the first evidence of female multitasking superiority.

Conversely, a Swedish study found that men actually outperformed women at handling multiple tasks simultaneously.

Impact On Human Happiness

Multitasking has been criticized as a hindrance to completing tasks or feeling happiness. Barry Schwartz has noted that, given the media-rich landscape of the Internet era, it is tempting to get into a habit of dwelling in a constant sea of information with too many choices, which has been noted to have a negative effect on human happiness.

Observers of youth in modern society often comment upon the apparently advanced multitasking capabilities of the youngest generations of humans. While it is true that contemporary researchers find that youths in today's world exhibit high levels of multitasking, most experts believe that members of the Net

Generation are not any better at multitasking than members of older generations.

How to Stop Multitasking

If we want to improve the quality of our work, lower our stress levels, and become more efficient, then we need get out of the multitasking habit. Below are some suggestions to help you cut back on multitasking:

• Plan your day in blocks. Set specific times for returning calls, answering emails, and doing research.

• Manage your interruptions . Keep a log showing who interrupts you the most, and how urgent the requests are. Once you've compiled a week's worth of interruptions, politely but assertively approach your colleagues with a view to managing and reducing their interruptions.

• Learn how to improve your concentration so you can focus properly on one task at a time. Doing this may feel awkward at first if you frequently multitask. But you'll be surprised at how much you get done just by concentrating on one thing at a time.

• Every time you go to check your email or take a call when you're actually supposed to be doing something else, take a deep breath and resist the urge. Focus your attention back to what you're supposed to be doing.

• If you get an audible or visual alert when emails come in, turn it off. This can help you avoid the temptation to check your inbox whenever you get new mail.

• Whenever you find yourself multitasking, stop. Take five minutes to sit quietly at your desk with your eyes closed. Even short breaks like this can refocus your mind, lower your stress levels, and improve your concentration. Plus it can give your brain a welcome break during a hectic day.

• There will be times when something urgent comes up and you can't avoid interruptions. But instead of trying to multitask through these, stop and make a note of where you left your current task. Record any thoughts you had about how to move forward. Then deal with the immediate problem, before going back to what you were doing. This way you'll be able to handle both tasks well, and you'll leave yourself with some clues to help you restart the original task more quickly.

• If you find your mind wandering when you should be focusing on something else, you need to guide your thoughts back to what you are doing by putting yourself in the moment. For example, you might be sitting in an important team meeting, but thinking about a speech you'll be giving soon. Tell yourself, "I am in this meeting, and need to focus on what I'm learning here." Often, acknowledging the moment can help keep you focused.

References:

"You say Multitasking like it's a good thing" by Charles J. Abate, March/April 2009 issue of NEAtoday

Wikipedia - Human Multitasking, http://en.wikipedia.org/wiki/Human_multitasking

IBM Operating System/360 Concepts and Facilities - Witt, Bernard I. & Lambert, Ward

"Is multi-tasking a myth?". BBC News August 20, 2010.

Hallowell, Edward M.. Crazy Busy: Overstretched, Overbooked, and About to Snap! Strategies for Handling Your Fast-Paced Life. 2007. Ballantine Books. ISBN 0-345-48244-1

Mayer, R. E., & Moreno, R. (2003). Nine ways to reduce cognitive load in multimedia learning. Educational Psychologist, 38(1), 43-52.

Junco, R. & Cotten, S. (2010). Perceived academic effects of instant messaging use. Computers & Education, 56(2), 370-378.

Junco, R. & Cotten, S. (2012). No A 4 U: The relationship between multitasking and academic performance. Computers & Education, 59(2), 505–514.

Wallis, Claudia (Mar 19, 2006). "The Multitasking Generation". Retrieved 4/26/10.

Lin, Lin (Sep 11, 2008). "Multitasking in Today's Learning Environment:Does Technology Make a Difference? University of North Texas.". Retrieved 4/26/10.

Rosen, Christine (2008). "The Myth of Multitasking". Retrieved 4/26/10.

Moran, Melanie (2009). "Training Can Improve Multitasking Ability". Retrieved 4/26/10.

Klingberg, Torkel (2009). The Overflowing Brain: Information Overload and the Limits of Working Memory. Oxford: Oxford UP. pp. 7, 8. ISBN 0-19-537288-3.

Adam Gorlick (2009). Media multitaskers pay mental price, Stanford study shows, Stanford Report, August 24, 2009.

Interview: Clifford Nass (Frontline)

Ophir, E., Nass, C. I., & Wagner, A. D. Cognitive control in media multitaskers. Proceedings of the National Academy of Sciences.

The Flow Model

The Optimum State of Performance And Productivity

Flow is the mental state of operation in which a person performing an activity is fully immersed in a feeling of energized focus, full involvement, and enjoyment in the process of the activity. In essence, flow is characterized by complete absorption in what one does. Proposed by Mihály Csíkszentmihályi, this positive psychology concept has been widely referenced across a variety of fields.

According to Csikszentmihalyi, flow is completely focused motivation. It is a single-minded immersion and represents perhaps the ultimate experience in harnessing the emotions in the service of performing and learning. In flow, the emotions are not just contained and channeled, but positive, energized, and aligned with the task at hand. To be caught in the ennui of depression or the agitation of anxiety is to be barred from flow.

The hallmark of flow is a feeling of spontaneous joy, even rapture, while performing a task although flow is also described as a deep focus on nothing but the activity – not even oneself or one's emotions.

Flow has many of the same positive characteristics as hyperfocus. However, hyperfocus is not always described in such universally glowing terms.

Let's take an example. Have you ever seen a hassled mom trying to get her young daughter to leave whatever she is doing and do something else?

It's a common enough sight: Young children can get so wrapped up in whatever they're doing that it takes a lot of persuasion to get them to switch their attention.

This ability to focus totally on one thing comes naturally to young children, but it's one of the biggest challenges that most of the rest of us face. We struggle to concentrate and, because of this, fail to get on with the work we're doing.

Some people, though, seem able to focus intensely on what they're doing, and perform exceptionally well as a result. Modern psychologists refer to this state of absolute absorption or concentration in what we are doing, as being "in flow."

According to Csikszentmihalyi, flow involves "being completely involved in an activity for its own sake. The ego falls away. Time flies. Every action, movement, and thought follows inevitably from the previous one, like playing jazz. Your whole being is involved, and you're using your skills to the utmost". So how do we enter this "ecstatic" state?

Components of Flow

Csíkszentmihályi identifies the following six factors as encompassing an experience of flow.

Intense and focused concentration on the present moment

Merging of action and awareness

A loss of reflective self-consciousness

A sense of personal control or agency over the situation or activity

A distortion of temporal experience, one's subjective experience of time is altered

Experience of the activity as intrinsically rewarding, also referred to as autotelic experience

Those aspects can appear independently of each other, but only in combination do they constitute a so-called flow experience.

State of Complete Absorption

Mihaly Csikszentmihalyi and his fellow researchers began researching flow after Csikszentmihalyi became fascinated by artists who would essentially get lost in their work. Artists, especially painters, got so immersed in their work that they would disregard their need for food, water and even sleep. Thus, the origin of research on the theory of flow came about when Csikszentmihalyi tried to understand this phenomenon experienced by these artists.

Flow research became prevalent in the 1980s and 1990s, with Csikszentmihalyi and his colleagues in Italy still at the forefront. Researchers interested in optimal experiences and emphasizing positive experiences, especially in places such as schools and the business world, also began studying the theory of flow at this time.

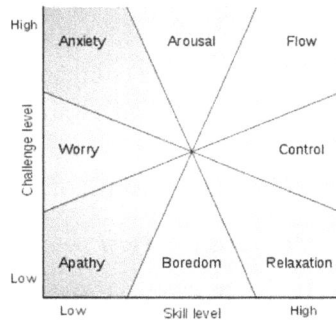

Flow has been experienced throughout history and across cultures. The teachings of Buddhism and Taoism speak of a state of mind known as the "action of inaction" or "doing without doing" that greatly resembles the idea of flow. Also, Indian texts on

> It is a question of absorption of thought. I have read in some paper that Mr. Stalin, the communist leader, he had to undergo a surgical operation of operating on the belly. But doctor wanted to, what is called, chloroform, but he said, "No, there is no need. You can go on with your operation." So even in ordinary life it is possible. Because the mind is absorbed in a different way, even a surgical operation does not disturb a man. Similarly, what to speak of spiritual life, if your mind is always absorbed in Krsna thought, Krsna consciousness...
> ~ Srila Prabhupada (Srimad-Bhagavatam 3.25.23 -- Bombay, November 23, 1974)

philosophy such as Ashtavakra Gita and the Yoga of Knowledge such as Bhagavad-Gita refer to a similar state.

Historical sources hint that Michelangelo may have painted the ceiling of the Vatican's Sistine Chapel while in a flow state. It is reported that he painted for days at a time, and he was so absorbed in his work that he did not even stop for food or sleep until he reached the point of passing out. After this, he would wake up refreshed and, upon starting to paint again, re-enter a state of complete absorption.

Bruce Lee either spoke of a psychological state similar to flow or spoke about the importance of adaptability and shedding preconceptions in his book the Tao of Jeet Kune Do.

In his book, he compares the state of flow to water where he so famously says, "Be like water ...If you put water into a cup, it becomes the cup. You put water into a bottle and it becomes the bottle. You put it in a teapot, it becomes the teapot. Be water, my friend."

Mechanism of Flow

In every given moment, there is a great deal of information made available to each individual. Psychologists have found that one's mind can attend to only a certain amount of information at a time. According to Mihaly's 1956 study, that number is about 126 bits of information per second. That may seem like a large number (and a lot of information), but simple daily tasks take quite a lot of information. Just having a conversation takes about 40 bits of information per second; that's 1/3 of one's capacity. That is why when having a conversation one cannot focus as much attention on other things.

For the most part (except for basic bodily feelings like hunger and pain, which are innate), people are able to decide what they want to focus their attention on. However, when one is in the flow state, he or she is completely engrossed with the one task at hand and, without making the conscious decision to do so, loses awareness of all other things: time, people, distractions, and even basic bodily needs. This occurs because all of the attention of the person in the flow state is on the task at hand; there is no more attention to be allocated.

Conditions for Flow

A flow state can be entered while performing any activity, although it is most likely to occur when one is wholeheartedly performing a task or activity for intrinsic purposes. Passive activities like taking a bath or even watching TV usually don't elicit flow experiences as individuals have to actively do something to enter a flow state.

Flow theory postulates three conditions that have to be met to achieve a flow state:

- One must be involved in an activity with a clear set of goals and progress. This adds direction and structure to the task.

- The task at hand must have clear and immediate feedback. This helps the person negotiate any changing demands and allows him or her to adjust his or her performance to maintain the flow state.

- One must have a good balance between the perceived challenges of the task at hand and his or her own perceived skills. One must have confidence in one's ability to complete the task at hand.

Schaffer (2013) proposed 7 flow conditions:

- Knowing what to do
- Knowing how to do it
- Knowing how well you are doing
- Knowing where to go (if navigation is involved)
- High perceived challenges
- High perceived skills
- Freedom from distractions

The autotelic personality

Csíkszentmihályi hypothesized that people with several very specific personality traits may be better able to achieve flow more often than the average person. These personality traits include curiosity, persistence, low self-centeredness, and a high rate of performing activities for intrinsic reasons only. People with most of these personality traits are said to have an autotelic personality.

Music

Musicians, especially improvisational soloists may experience a similar state of mind while playing their instrument. Research has shown that performers in a flow state have a heightened quality of performance as opposed to when they are not in a flow state.

In a study performed with professional classical pianists who played piano pieces several times to induce a flow state, a significant relationship was found between the flow state of the pianist and the pianist's heart rate, blood pressure, and major facial muscles. As the pianist entered the flow state, heart rate and blood pressure decreased and the major facial muscles relaxed.

This study further emphasized that flow is a state of effortless attention. In spite of the effortless attention and overall relaxation of the body, the performance of the pianist during the flow state improved.

Groups of drummers experience a state of flow when they sense a collective energy that drives the beat, something they refer to as getting into the groove. Bass guitarists often describe a state of flow when properly playing between the percussion and melody as being in the pocket.

Sports

The concept of being in the zone during an athletic performance fits within Csíkszentmihályi's description of the flow experience, and theories and applications of being in the zone and its relationship with athletic competitive advantage are topics studied in the field of sport psychology.

Mixed martial arts champion and Karate master Lyoto Machida uses meditation techniques before fights to attain mushin, a concept that, by his description, is in all respects equal to flow.

Flow In The Workplace

Flow is easiest to achieve when:

• You have enough pressure on you to stay engaged, but not so much that it's harming your performance.

• You believe that your skills are good enough to perform well.

• You have distraction under control.

• You are attending to the task in hand, rather than analyzing and critiquing your performance.

• You are relaxed and alert.

• You are thinking positively, and have eliminated all negative thoughts.

Some of these are hard to achieve in a busy office environment. Your phone rings, your e-mail beeps to indicate that a new message has arrived, and co-workers pop by to ask you questions. At the same time you can't stop thinking about a whole range of personal and work issues that are causing you stress, not least of which is the sheer quantity of work which is piling up.

So if you're to have a good chance of getting into flow, you need to sort out all of these distractions first. Here are some practical things you can do:

• Get comfortable, and eliminate distraction from your environment. Rearrange your working environment so that you eliminate as many distractions as possible. Change the orientation of your desk, so that people passing don't distract you. Use plants and screens to damp noise. Adjust furniture so that it's comfortable. If untidiness distracts you, tidy up. Make sure the temperature is comfortable, and that your work area is well lit.

• Keep interruptions at bay. Put up the "Do not disturb" sign, switch off your cell phone, close your email reader and web browser, and do anything that will block the most common things that distract you from work. You'll be surprised at how much you can get done in just one hour of uninterrupted work, which may be the equivalent of plodding on for several hours if you're handling interruptions at the same time.

With all of that in place, you can start to practice your concentration skills. Try to focus on one task at a time to the exclusion of others, as far as you can.

Religion And spirituality

Csíkszentmihályi may have been the first to describe this concept in Western psychology, but as he himself readily acknowledges he was most certainly not the first to quantify the concept of flow or develop applications based on the concept.

For millennia, practitioners of Eastern religions such as Hinduism, Buddhism and Taoism have honed the discipline of overcoming the duality of self and object as a central feature of spiritual development. Eastern spiritual practitioners have developed a very thorough and holistic set of theories around overcoming duality of self and object, tested and refined through spiritual practice instead of the systematic rigor and controls of modern science.

Chabad-Hasidic Jewish philosophy also encourages that "the action is the main thing" and that a person must have a strong sense of Divine mission to elevate the world that transcends all other needs, and that a sense of self detracts from a sense of the Divine. It emphasizes the tension between the Divine soul and the animal soul in accomplishing this flow.

Practitioners of the varied schools of Zen Buddhism apply concepts similar to flow to aid their mastery of art forms, including, in the case of Japanese Zen Buddhism, Aikido, Cheng Hsin, Judo, Honkyoku, Kendo and Ikebana.

In yogic traditions such as Raja Yoga reference is made to a state of flow in the practice of Samyama, a psychological absorption in the object of meditation. Theravada Buddhism refers to "access concentration," which is a state of flow achieved through meditation and used to further strengthen concentration.

In Islam the first mental state that precedes human action is known as al-khatir. In this state an image or thought is born in the mind. When in this mental state and contemplating upon an ayat or an imprint of God, one may experience a profound state or flow whereby the phenomena of nature, the macrocosmic world and the souls of people are understood as a sign of God.

References:

Mihaly Csikszentmihalyi (1990). Flow: The Psychology of Optimal Experience. Harper & Row. ISBN 978-0-06-016253-5. Retrieved 10 November 2013.

Wikipedia Flow (Psychology)

Daniel Goleman (12 September 1996). Emotional Intelligence: Why It Can Matter More Than IQ. Bloomsbury. p. 91. ISBN 978-0-7475-2830-2. Retrieved 10 November 2013.

Nakamura, J.; Csikszentmihalyi, M. (20 December 2001). "Flow Theory and Research". In C. R. Snyder Erik Wright, and Shane J. Lopez. Handbook of Positive Psychology. Oxford University Press. pp. 195–206. ISBN 973-0-19-803094-2. Retrieved 20 November 2013.

Mihály Csíkszentmihályi (1975). Beyond boredom and anxiety. Jossey-Bass Publishers. pp. 10–. ISBN 978-0-7879-5140-5. Retrieved 10 November 2013.

Schwartz, Robert C. (April 12, 2004). "No way is way: The power of artistry in psychotherapy.". Annals Of The American Psychotherapy 6(1) (1535-4075): 18–21.

Csikszentmihalyi, M. (1988), "The flow experience and its significance for human psychology", in Csikszentmihalyi, M , Optimal experience: psychological studies of flow in consciousness, Cambridge, UK: Cambridge University Press, pp. 15–35, ISBN 978-0-521-43809-4

Csikszentmihalyi, M., Finding Flow, 1997.

Snyder, C.R. & Lopez, S.J. (2007), Positive psychology: The scientific and practical explorations of human strengths, London, UK: Sage Publications

Csikszentmihalyi, M., Larson, R., & Prescott, S. (1977). The ecology of adolescent activity and experience. Journal of Youth and Adolescence, 6, 281-294.

Delle Fave, A., & Bassi, M. (2000). The quality of experience in adolescents' daily lives: Developmental perspectives. Genetic, Social, and General Psychology Monographs, 126, 347-367.

Csikszentmihalyi, M.; Abuhamdeh, S. & Nakamura, J. (2005), "Flow", in Elliot, A., Handbook of Competence and Motivation, New York: The Guilford Press, pp. 598–698

Keller, J., & Landhäußer, A. (2012). The flow model revisited. In S. Engeser (Ed.), Advances in flow research (pp. 51-64). New York: Springer.

Moneta, G. B. (2012). On the measurement and conceptualization of flow. In S. Engeser (Ed.), Advances in flow research (pp. 23-50). New York: Springer.

Ellis, G. D., Voelkl, J. E., & Morris, C. (1994). Measurement and analysis issues with explanation of variance in daily experience using the flow model. Journal of Leisure Research, 26, 337.

Haworth, John; Stephen Evans (November 14, 2011). "Challenge, skill and positive subjective states in the daily life of a sample of YTS students.". Journal Of Occupational And Organizational Psychology. 68(2) (2044-8325): 109–121. doi:10.1111/j.2044-8325.1995.tb00576.x.

Interruptions

The average American worker has fifty interruptions a day, of which seventy percent have nothing to do with work. Avoid interruptions to save time.

Interruptions In Office Work

Some office workers use so many computer programs at once that they have to use two screens.

According to Gloria Mark, a leader in interruption science, the average knowledge worker switches tasks every three minutes, and, once distracted, a worker takes nearly a half-hour to resume the original task."

Gloria Mark conducted a study on office workers, which revealed that "each employee spent only 11 minutes on any given project before being interrupted" and that it took, "on average, 25 minutes to return" to their initial task. At the same time, Mark's study indicated that constant e-mail interruptions are also an important source of information for office workers.

A study indicates that "employers seeking to decrease interruptions may want to have their workers use instant messaging software". The study showed that "workers who used instant messaging on the job reported less interruption than colleagues who did not". Even though "using instant messaging led to more conversations on the computer, ...the conversations were briefer".

Interruptions to Pilots and Health care Professionals

Pilots are surrounded by gauges, meters, lights and switches and they get voice messages both in person, from members of their flight crew, and on their radios, from air traffic controllers.

When surgeons are performing operations, interruptions or distractions could have a serious impact.

For professions such as jet pilots, astronauts, or surgeons in the operating room, interruptions at the wrong time could even have major consequences. Mary Czerwinski, "one of the world's leading experts in interruption science" helps "NASA design the information systems for the International Space Station". She has to try to figure out how to "deliver an interruption to a busy astronaut" regarding mechanical errors without being "too distracting, because it could throw off the astronauts and cause them to mess up million-dollar experiments".

In nursing, a study has been conducted of the impact of interruptions on nurses in a trauma center. Another study has been done on the interruption rates of nurses and doctors.

Interruption caused by smart phone use in health care settings can be deadly. Hence, it may be worthwhile for health care organizations to craft effective cell phone usage policies to maximize technological benefits and minimize unnecessary distraction associated with smart phone use.

Interruptions And Distractions

Everyday interruptions at work can be a key barrier to managing your time effectively and, ultimately, can be a barrier to your success.

Think back to your last workday, and consider for a minute the many interruptions that occurred. There may have been phone calls, emails, hallway conversations, colleagues stopping by your office, or anything else that unexpectedly demanded your attention and, in doing so, distracted you from the task at-hand.

Because your day only has so many hours in it, a handful of small interruptions can rob you of the time you need to achieve your goals and be successful in your work and life.

More than this, they can break your focus, meaning that you have to spend time re-engaging with the thought processes needed to successfully complete complex work.

The key to controlling interruptions is to know what they are and whether they are necessary, and to plan for them in your daily schedule. The tips that follow will help you do that, and so prevent interruptions from frustrating you and jeopardizing your success.

How Often Are You Distracted At Work?

It's a question that's almost laughable, right? Most of us are distracted several times, if not dozens of times, every day.

We get emergency emails and phone calls. We take breaks to browse the Internet. Co-workers walk into our office for a quick chat, or send us amusing instant messages.

It doesn't matter where you work or what you do, you probably deal with distractions on a daily basis. And these distractions are costly: a 2007 study by Basex estimated that distractions cost U.S. businesses $588 billion per year, and this high cost is likely repeated in organizations around the world.

What's more (and depending on the complexity of our work), regaining concentration after a distraction can take quite a few minutes. If we're distracted 10 times a day, multiply the time lost by 10, and it's easy to see why we sometimes don't get much quality work done.

Learning how to minimize distractions can dramatically increase your productivity and effectiveness, as well as reduce your stress.

Without distractions, you can get into flow, produce high-quality work, and achieve much more during the day.

Sometimes You Need To Stay In Touch But Be Out Of Reach.

• If your colleague loves to gossip all afternoon, then don't make it easy for him. When he comes into your office, stand up – and don't sit back down until he leaves. You can also keep a stack of books on your office chair so he can't sit down.

• While office small talk, gossip, and casual conversations are an important part of relationship building, try to stay in your office when you have a lot of work to do. This way, you won't run into others who want to talk when you don't

"For those of you headed to the office, today's forecast calls for scattered frustration, followed by a brief storm of criticism and a flurry of random distractions."

have time. If you must leave your office, and then colleagues pull you aside, make sure you tell them where you're going. For example, you can say, "Is this going to be quick? I'm on my way to a meeting."

Windows, a busy highway, or loud co-workers may all contribute to a distracting work environment.

• Work in another location – If possible, work in a conference room or empty office to regain your concentration. If your job allows it, working in a different setting, such as at home, or a library, may also help you to focus more.

• Use "white noise" – If noise is a problem, install padded partitions, or consider buying a sound machine that produces white noise to cover annoying sounds. Noise-canceling headphones with soft music can also improve your focus. You can also download white noise files from the Internet and set them on "repeat." Having white noise play constantly helps block unwanted sounds.

Other People

Co-workers often create the greatest distractions.

• Close your door – Close your office door to keep people from casually stopping by. If they knock or come in anyway, explain that when your door is closed, you shouldn't be disturbed unless there's an emergency. A sign on your office door may also help. (If you're a manager, there's clearly a tension between this and – very importantly – making sure that your "door is always open" to members of your team. Consider working from home or in a conference room when you don't want to be disturbed.)

• Use headphones – If you're in a cubicle or open office environment, people are less likely to interrupt you if you're wearing headphones. (You don't even have to be listening to music!)

• Talk to the disrupter – If you share an office with someone who often disrupts your day, talk to the person about the problem: he may not realize he's distracting you.

"Available" and "Unavailable" Time

Simple yet effective: Let people know when you are available. and when you are not. Make sure that people know that during your "unavailable time", they should only interrupt you if they have to.

Those who are enlightened know that this is a miserable condition, whereas others say, "That is all right." "We are enjoying very nicely." In this way we are being kicked, like a football, thrown first to the party of lust and then to the party of anger. If the football thinks, "I am free, I am moving of my own accord," what is that freedom? Simply the freedom to be kicked; as the ball is kicked by the player, so we are being kicked by the power of lust and anger, the concomitants of material nature.
~ Srila Prabhupada (Man's Link to God)

You and your co-workers can also agree on a signal that everyone in the office can use when unavailable, like turning the nameplate on the door around, or simply closing the door. This alleviates interruptions and can avoid hurt feelings.

Uncontrollable Interruptions

There are interruptions that, no matter how hard you try, you simply cannot control.

Most people are happy to schedule a more convenient time, but when this does not work, quickly set the parameters by saying something like, "I only have five minutes to talk about this right now," and stick to it.

Do not ask the interrupter to sit down and do not engage in small talk. Encourage the interrupter to get right to the point and if a solution cannot be reached before the allotted time runs out, set a time for getting back to them and, again, stick to it.

Keep An Interrupters Log

If interruptions consistently rob you of time and energy, or if they frequently push you off schedule and cause delays, it's time to keep an Interrupters Log. This is a simple record of the interruptions you experience in the course of a day.

It can have the following columns:
Person

> *This example is given in the Srimad-Bhagavatam that just like we have got our senses, similarly, if somebody has got several wives, so one wife is snatching him that: "You come to my room," another wife is snatching: "You come to my room." So he's perplexed. Similarly we have got these wives, the senses. The eyes are dragging: "Please come to the cinema." The tongue is dragging: "Please come to the restaurant." The hand is driving somewhere else. The leg is driving somewhere. So our position is like that. The same man, who has got different wives and dragging him to different room. This is our position.*
>
> *~ Srila Prabhuapda (Bhagavad-gita 2.8 -- London, August 8, 1973)*

Date and Time
Description of Interruption
Valid?
Urgent?

Keep your Interrupters Log with you every day for at least a week, recording every interruption you experience, and marking down the person interrupting you; the date and time it occurs; what the interruption is; whether it was valid; and whether it was urgent (or whether someone could have waited until a better time.)

Once you have recorded the interruptions for a week, sit down with your log and analyze the information.

Analyze and Conquer Interruptions

To analyze and conquer the interruptions you find in your Interrupters Log, firstly look at whether the interruption is valid or not.

Could someone have avoided interrupting you by waiting for a routine meeting? Or was it something they should have asked you about at all?

If not, deal with this politely but assertively .

"Maybe I haven't made myself clear enough. I really don't want to be disturbed today."

Next, look at how urgent the interruptions were, and whether they could have been pre-empted. You can pre-empt many interruptions by holding routine meetings with people: If they're confident that they'll have access to you at a defined point in the near future, *they'll learn to save up non-urgent issues until this meeting.*

However, some interruptions are both urgent and valid. You need to be interrupted, and you need to deal with the situation.

From your Interrupters Log, you'll see how much time is taken up by these urgent, valid interruptions. Block this time into your schedule as "contingency time", and only take on as much other work as you can fit into the remaining time. You'll have to juggle this other work around the interruptions, but at least you won't be overloaded and stressed by the things that you haven't done because they've been displaced by emergencies.

Which Interruptions Are Valid And Which Are Not?

You need to deal with the valid interruptions.

As for the interruptions that are not valid, you must find a way to block these out in the future.

Put Your Phone to Work for You (Not Against You)

A little bit of planning can go a long way in working to control telephone interruptions, which many people experience all day long. If you are on a deadline or your focus needs to be intense (and not interrupted), use your voice mail to screen calls, or have an assistant deal with messages for you. This way, you can deal with calls by priority, and at times that suit you. In fact, this telephone time can be planned into your schedule, and so become a normal part of your working day.

Reference:

Interruption Science': Costly Distractions at Work October 14, 2005 http://www.npr.org/templates/story/story.php?storyId=4958831 Accessed on June 18, 2011

Carroll, John M. "Notification and awareness: synchronizing task-oriented collaborative activity". International Journal of Human-Computer Studies. 16 October 2012.

Iqbal, Shamsi T. "Oasis: A Framework for Linking Notification Delivery to the Perceptual Structure of Goal-Directed Tasks". Microsoft Research. Microsoft. 17 October 2012.

McCrickard, D. Scott; Czerwinski, Bartram (May 2003). "Introduction: Design and evaluation of notification user interfaces.". International Journal of Human-Computer Studies 58 (5): 6. doi:10.1016/S1071-5819(03)00025-9. 17 October 2012.

Jackson, Thomas; Dawson, Wilson (April 2002). "Case study: evaluating the effect of email interruptions within the workplace". Conference on Empirical Assessment in Software Engineering: 3–7. 17 October 2012.

Thompson, Clive (16 October 2005). "Meet the Life Hackers". The New York Times. 17 October 2012.

Iqbal, Shamsi T.; Horvitz (2010). "Notifications and awareness: a field study of alert usage and preferences". Proceedings of the 2010 ACM Conference on Computer Supported Cooperative Work: 27–30. doi:10.1145/1718918.1718926. 17 October 2012.

Bhatia, S; McCrickard (2006). "Listening to your inner voices: Investigating means for voice notifications". Proceedings of the SIGCHI Conference on Human Factors in Computing Systems. 17 October 2012.

Iqbal, Shamsi T; Bailey (2008). "Effects of Intelligent Notification Management on Users and Their Tasks". Proceeding of the Twenty-Sixth Annual SIGCHI Conference on Human Factors in Computing Systems, CHI'08: 93–102. 17 October 2012.

Cutrell, Edward; Czerwinski, Horvitz (2001). "Notification, Disruption, and Memory: Effects of Messaging Interruptions on Memory and Performance". INTERACT 2001 Conference Proceedings: 263–269. 17 October 2012.

Roda, Claudia (2011). Human attention and its implications for human–computer interaction. Cambridge: Cambridge University Press. pp. 11–62.

Marci Alboher. "Fighting a War Against Distraction". New York Times. June 22, 2008

"Meet the Life Hackers" by Clive Thompson. October 16, 2005, web: NYT6.

Instant Messaging Proves Useful In Reducing Workplace Interruption ScienceDaily (June 4, 2008) http://www.sciencedaily.com/releases/2008/06/080603120251.htm

Pomodoro Technique

Using Interruption Creatively

The Pomodoro Technique is a time management method developed by Francesco Cirillo in the late 1980s. The technique uses a timer to break down work into intervals traditionally 25 minutes in length, separated by short breaks. These intervals are known as "pomodori", the plural of the Italian word pomodoro for "tomato". The method is based on the idea that frequent breaks can improve mental agility.

The "Pomodoro Technique" is named after the tomato-shaped kitchen timer that was first used by Cirillo when he was a university student.

Underlying Principles

There are five basic steps to implementing the technique:
Decide on the task to be done
Set the pomodoro timer to n minutes (traditionally 25)
Work on the task until the timer rings; record with an x
Take a short break (3-5 minutes)
Every four "pomodori" take a longer break (15–30 minutes)
The stages of planning, tracking, recording, processing and visualizing are fundamental to the technique.

In the planning phase tasks are prioritized by recording them in a "To Do Today" list. This enables users to estimate the effort tasks require. As "pomodori" are completed, they are recorded, adding to a sense of accomplishment and providing raw data for subsequent self-observation and improvement.

For the purposes of the technique, "pomodoro" refers to the interval of time spent working. After task completion, any time remaining in the "pomodoro" is devoted to overlearning. Regular breaks are taken, aiding assimilation. A short (3-5 minute) rest separates consecutive "pomodori". Four "pomodori" form a set. A longer (15-30 minute) rest is taken between sets.

An essential aim of the technique is to reduce the impact of internal and external interruptions on focus and flow. A "pomodoro" is indivisible. When interrupted during a "pomodoro" either the other activity must be recorded and postponed (inform – negotiate – schedule – call back) or the "pomodoro" must be abandoned.

Tools

The creator and others encourage a low-tech approach, using a mechanical timer, paper and pencil. The physical act of winding up the timer confirms the user's determination to start the task; ticking externalises desire to complete the task; ringing announces a break. Flow and focus become associated with these physical stimuli.

The technique has inspired application software for a variety of platforms, such as the "focus booster" app, which was first developed in 2010.

References:

Cirillo, Francesco. The Pomodoro Technique.

Cirillo, Francesco. "The Pomodoro Technique (The Pomodoro)".

Shellenbarger, Sue (2009-11-18). ""Shellenbarger, Sue" (November 2009) The Wall Street Journal - "Testing Time Management Strategies"". Online.wsj.com.

"Tambini, Arielle; Ketz, Nicholas; Davachi, Lila" "Enhanced Brain Correlations during Rest Are Related to Memory for Recent Experiences" Neuron (January 2010)". Cell.com.

Olsen, Patricia R. (September 2009) The New York Times- "For Writing Software, a Buddy System"

Big Rocks Go In First

One day an expert was speaking to a group of business students about time management. He pulled out a one-gallon, wide-mouthed mason jar and set it on a table in front of him. Then he produced about a dozen fist-sized rocks and carefully placed them, one at a time, into the jar.

When the jar was filled to the top and no more rocks would fit inside, he asked, "Is this jar full?" Everyone in the class said, "Yes."

Then he said, "Really?" He reached under the table and pulled out a bucket of gravel. Then he dumped some gravel in and shook the jar causing pieces of gravel to work themselves down into the spaces between the big rocks.

Then he asked the group once more, "Is the jar full?" By this time the class was onto him. "Probably not," one of them answered.

"Good!" he replied. He reached under the table and brought out a bucket of sand. He started dumping the sand in and it went into all the spaces left between the rocks and the gravel. Once more he asked the question, "Is this jar full?"

"No!" the class shouted. Once again he said, "Good!" Then he grabbed a pitcher of water and began to pour it in until the jar was filled to the brim. Then he looked up at the class and asked, "What is the point of this illustration?"

One student raised their hand and said, "The point is, no matter how full your schedule is, if you try really hard, you can always fit some more things into it!"

"No," the speaker replied, "that's not the point. The truth this illustration teaches us is, if you don't put the big rocks in first, you'll never get them in at all."

In both our business and personal lives, we have big rocks, sand, gravel and water. The natural tendency is to favor the latter three elements, leaving little space for the big rocks.

In an effort to respond to the urgent, the important is sometimes set aside.

Make a list of your big rocks. Then make a plant to ensure that big rocks are put first. Block out the time in your schedule for these activities. Amazingly the other stuff still gets done.

Big rocks are important life goals. Unless you put them in your time-slot, the inevitable sand and water issues will fill up your days and you won't be able to fit the important life goals.

In conclusion, one should not waste his time by so-called economic development and sense gratification, but should cultivate spiritual knowledge to understand the Supersoul and the individual soul and their relationship. In this way, by advancement of knowledge, one can achieve liberation and the ultimate goal of life. It is said that if one takes to the path of liberation, even rejecting his so-called duties in the material world, he is not a loser at all. But a person who does not take to the path of liberation yet carefully executes economic development and sense gratification loses everything.

~ Srila Prabhuapda (Srimad Bhagavatam 4.22.37)

Don't Confuse Activity

With Productivity

Thriving on "Busy"

Some people get a rush from being busy. The narrowly-met deadlines, the endless emails, the piles of files needing attention on the desk, the frantic race to the meeting... What an adrenaline buzz!

The problem is that an "addiction to busyness" rarely means that you're effective, and it can lead to stress.

Instead, try to slow down, and learn to manage your time better.

Our Culture Is Obsessed With Being Busy

We're suffering, as you know, from an epidemic of busyness. But even more than that, we're suffering from an epidemic of people talking about how busy they are. Moaning about one's schedule has become, for some, a mark of social status. Let's call this phenomenon 'busy-bragging'.

Often many of us who engage in it are doing it consciously to impress others. But for some others, those busy feelings are real. The real culprit is a socioeconomic system that relentlessly instrumentalises everyone, forcing us to become productivity machines, valued by our output alone.

It's Glamorous To Be Busy

When you ask anyone how they're doing, often the default response is: "Busy!" "So busy." "Crazy busy." It is, pretty obviously, a boast disguised as a complaint. And the stock response is a kind of congratulation: "That's a good problem to have," or "Better than the opposite."

It's almost always people whose lamented busyness is purely self-imposed: work and obligations they've taken on voluntarily, classes and activities they've "encouraged" their kids to participate in. They're busy because of their own ambition or drive or anxiety, because they're addicted to busyness and dread what they might have to face in its absence.

These people feel anxious and guilty when they aren't either working or doing something to promote their work.

Even Kids Are Into This Hysteria

Even children are busy now, scheduled down to the half-hour with classes and extracurricular activities. They come home at the end of the day as tired as grown-ups.

The present hysteria is not a necessary or inevitable condition of life; it's something we've chosen.

Inayam deho deha-bhajam nr-loke
kastan kaman arhate vid-bhujam ye
tapo divyam putraka yena sattvam
suddhyed yasmad brahma-saukhyam tv anantam

"My dear sons, there is no reason to labor very hard for sense pleasure while in this human form of life; such pleasures are available to the stool-eaters [hogs]. Rather, you should undergo penances in this life by which your existence will be purified, and as a result you will be able to enjoy unlimited transcendental bliss."
~Srimad-Bhagavatam also (5.5.1)

Our Frantic Days Are Really Just A Hedge Against Emptiness.

Busyness serves as a kind of existential reassurance, a hedge against emptiness; obviously your life cannot possibly be silly or trivial or meaningless if you are so busy, completely booked, in demand every hour of the day.

More and more people no longer make or do anything tangible; all this histrionic exhaustion is a way of covering up the fact that most of what we do doesn't matter.

Disciple: They say we are escaping from reality.

Srila Prabhupada: Yes, we are escaping their reality. But their reality is a dog's race, and our reality is to advance in self-realization, Krsna consciousness. That is the difference. Therefore the mundane, materialistic workers have been described as mudhas, asses. Why? Because the ass works very hard for no tangible gain. He carries on his back tons of cloth for the washerman, and the washerman in return gives him a little morsel of grass. Then the ass stands at the washerman's door, eating the grass, while the washerman loads him up again. The ass has no sense to think, "If I get out of the clutches of this washerman, I can get grass anywhere. Why am I carrying so much?"

The mundane workers are like that. They're busy at the office, very busy. If you want to see the fellow, "I am very busy now." [Laughter.] So what is the result of your being so busy? "Well, I take two pieces of toast and one cup of tea. That's all." [Laughter.] And for this purpose you are so busy?

Or, he is busy all day simply so that in the evening he can look at his account books and say, "Oh, the balance had been one thousand dollars -- now it has become two thousand." That is his satisfaction. But still he will have the same two pieces of bread and one cup of tea, even though he has increased his balance from one thousand to two thousand. And still he'll work hard. This is why karmis are called mudhas. They work like asses, without any real aim of life.

But Vedic civilization is different. The accusation implied in the question is not correct. In the Vedic system, people are not lazy. They are very busy working for a higher purpose.

~ Srila Prabhupada (Progressing Beyond "Progress")

Life Is Too Short To Be 'Busy'

Idleness is not just a vacation, an indulgence or a vice; it is as indispensable to the brain as vitamin D is to the body, and deprived of it we suffer a mental affliction as disfiguring as rickets. The space and quiet that idleness provides is a necessary condition for standing back from life and seeing it whole, for making unexpected connections and waiting for the wild summer lightning strikes of inspiration — it is, paradoxically, necessary to getting any work done. "Idle dreaming is often of the essence of what we do," wrote Thomas Pynchon in his essay on sloth. Archimedes' "Eureka" in the bath, Newton's apple, Jekyll & Hyde and the benzene ring: history is full of stories of inspirations

> I had this wonderful dream that I slept for eight solid hours— but then I woke up.

In Germany, I think, or somewhere there is classification: "Lazy intelligent, busy intelligent, lazy fool, and busy fool." So at the present moment (laughs) the whole world is full of busy fools. But the first-class man, he is lazy intelligent. Lazy and intelligent, that is first-class man. And second-class man, busy intelligent. And third class means lazy fool and fourth class means busy fool. When the fools are busy... Just like nowadays they are busy but they are fools. Like monkey, he is very busy. You see? And they prefer to be generation of monkey, busy fool. That's all. Fools, when he is busy, he is simply creating havoc. That's all. Better... Lazy fool is better than him because he will not create so much harm, but this busy fool will simply create harm. And first class-man is lazy intelligent. He knows the value of life, and soberly he is thinking. Just like all our great saintly persons. They were living in the forest, meditation, tapasya, and writing books. They are first-class men.
> ~ Srila Prabhupada (Morning Walk -- October 19, 1975, Johannesburg)

that come in idle moments and dreams. It almost makes you wonder whether loafers, goldbricks and no-accounts aren't responsible for more of the world's great ideas, inventions and masterpieces than the hardworking.

Action: Eliminate All Unnecessary Tasks

Think about all of the tasks that you complete on a weekly basis, and eliminate the ones that can be deemed as being unnecessary. Eliminate the "clutter" in your weekly schedule and free up some time.

You're really not as busy as you think. Try this exercise, and you'll have some time to do that something that you want to.

'I haven't the slightest idea who he is. He came bundled with the software.'

Action: Stop Taking On Extra Unneeded Tasks

People often take on unneeded tasks, and then complain that they are too busy to do something. You have to get rid of anything in your schedule that is unneeded If you want to "unbusy" yourself.

This may include tasks like volunteering as a coach for a children's soccer team or working extra hours when you are not in need of the extra money.

You can eliminate some of these unneeded tasks and have more than enough time to do the something that you want to do.

At the end of the day it's about weighing them out. Figure out whether you view the unneeded task or the something that you want to do as being more important and your decision will practically be made for you!

Just get rid of some clutter in your schedule and you'll have more time!

Action: Put Yourself First...

Value yourself over the things that you own. Treat your body at least as well as you treat your car. People are more conscious of their possessions than their very self.

A person opened the door of his BMW, when suddenly a car came along and hit the door, ripping it off completely. When the police arrived at the scene, the person was complaining bitterly about the damage to his precious BMW. "Officer, look what they've done to my Beeeemer!!!", he whined.

"You people are so materialistic, you make me sick!" retorted the officer, "You're so worried about your stupid BMW, that you didn't even notice that your left arm was ripped off!!!"

"Oh my gaaad....", screamed the person, finally noticing the bloody left shoulder where his arm once was, "Where's my Rolex watch???!!!!!"

Implement these 3 actions today and you'll get rid of some clutter within your schedule and free up some time to do the "something" that you desire!

References:

Oliver Burkeman, The Guardian, March 24, 2014

Michael Cimicata, Passive Income Journey.

Ian Lang, Why It's OK To Stop Pretending To Be Busy

Tim Kreider, June, 2012, The New York Times

Hanna Rosin, You're Not As Busy As You Say You Are

To-Do Lists

The Key to Efficiency

Do you often feel overwhelmed by the amount of work you have to do, or do you find yourself missing deadlines? Or do you sometimes just forget to do something important, so that people have to chase you to get work done?

All of these are symptoms of not keeping a proper "To-Do List." To-Do Lists are prioritized lists of all the tasks that you need to carry out. They list everything that you have to do, with the most important tasks at the top of the list, and the least important tasks at the bottom.

By keeping a To-Do List, you make sure that your tasks are written down all in one place so you don't forget anything important. And by prioritizing tasks, you plan the order in which you'll do them, so that you can tell what needs your immediate attention, and what you can leave until later.

To-Do Lists are essential if you're going to beat work overload. When you don't use To-Do Lists effectively, you'll appear unfocused and unreliable to the people around you. When you do use them effectively, you'll be much better organized, and you'll be much more reliable. You'll experience less stress, safe in the knowledge that you haven't forgotten anything important. More than this, if you prioritize intelligently, you'll focus your time and energy on high value activities, which will mean that you're more productive, and more valuable to your team.

Keeping a properly structured and thought-out To-Do List sounds simple enough. But it can be surprising how many people fail to use To-Do Lists at all, never mind use them effectively. In fact, it's often when people start to use To-Do Lists effectively and sensibly that they make their first personal productivity breakthroughs, and start making a success of their careers.

Preparing a To-Do List

Writing your list down on paper or putting it into a document is the simplest and easiest way to start using To-Do Lists. Then follow these steps:

Step 1:

Write down all of the tasks that you need to complete. If they're large tasks, break out the first action step, and write this down with the larger task. (Ideally, tasks or action steps should take no longer than 1-2 hours to complete.)

Note:

You may find it easier to compile several lists (personal, study, and workplace To-Do Lists, for example). Try different approaches and use the best for your own situation.

Step 2:

Run through these tasks allocating priorities from A (very important, or very urgent) to F (unimportant, or not at all urgent).

If too many tasks have a high priority, run through the list again and demote the less important ones. Once you have done this, rewrite the list in priority order.

Using Your To-Do Lists

To use your To-Do List, simply work your way through it in order, dealing with the A priority tasks first, then the Bs, then the Cs, and so on. As you complete tasks, tick them off or strike them through.

You can use To-Do Lists in different ways in different situations. For instance, if you're in a sales-type role, a good way to motivate yourself is to keep your To-Do List relatively short, and aim to complete it every day.

In you're in an operational role, or if tasks are large or dependent on too many other people, then it may be better to focus on a longer-term list, and "chip away" at it day-by-day.

THINGS TO DO TODAY

Date_____ COMPLETED

1) _____ ☐
2) _____ ☐
3) _____ ☐
4) _____ ☐
5) _____ ☐
6) _____ ☐
7) _____ ☐
8) _____ ☐
9) _____ ☐
10) _____ ☐

Many people find it helpful to spend, say, 10 minutes at the end of the day, organizing tasks on their To-Do List for the next day.

Tip:

Once you're comfortable using To-Do Lists, you can start differentiating between urgency and importance.

Using Software

Although using a paper list is an easy way to get started using To-Do Lists, software-based approaches can be more efficient in spite of the learning curve. These can remind you of events or tasks that will soon be overdue, they can also be synchronized with your phone or email, and they can be shared with others on your team, if you're collaborating on a project.

> *Time is compared herein to a sharp razor. A razor is meant to shave the hair from one's face, but if not carefully handled, the razor will cause disaster. One is advised not to create a disaster by misusing his lifetime. One should be extremely careful to utilize the span of his life ....*
> *~ Srila Prabhupada (Srimad Bhagavatam 6.5.19)*

There are many time management software programs available. At a simple level, you can use MSWord or MSExcel to manage your To-Do Lists. Some versions of Microsoft Outlook, and other email services such as Gmail, have task lists and To-Do Lists as standard features. Remember the Milk is another popular online task management tool that will sync with your smartphone, PDA, or email account. It can even show you where your To-Do List tasks are on a map. Other similar services include Todoist and Toodledo.

One of the biggest advantages to using a software-based approach to manage your To-Do List is that you can update it easily. For example, instead of scratching off tasks and rewriting the list every day, software allows you to move and prioritize tasks quickly.

Tip:

All of us think, plan and work differently. A program that works well for a colleague might not work well for you simply because you learn and think in your own way. This is why it's useful to research and try several different ways of compiling your To-Do List before deciding on a single system.

Examples

To-Do Lists can help you stay on top of important projects and piles of undone tasks or decisions.

labdhva sudurlabham idam bahu-sambhavante
manusyam arthadam anityam apiha dhirah
turnam yateta na pated anu mrtyu yavan
nihsreyasaya visayah khalu sarvatah syat
"This human form of life is obtained after many, many births, and although it is not permanent, it can offer the highest benefits. Therefore a sober and intelligent man should immediately try to fulfill his mission and attain the highest profit in life before another death occurs. He should avoid sense gratification, which is available in all circumstances."
~ Srimad-Bhagavatam (11.9.29)

For instance, imagine you're heading a team that's working on a large, complex project. There are so many tasks to do, and so many people doing them, that staying on top of it all seems overwhelming.

You can use a To-Do List in this situation to help stay organized. You can structure your list by team member, writing out tasks and deadlines for every person on the project. Each day as you write out your own tasks that need completion, you can also check your Team To-Do List to see who's working on what, and if anything is due in that day. You can also include other tasks that you need to complete as part of your job.

Or, imagine you're in a sales role and have a long list of people who you need to talk to. You write out a list of everyone you need to call and every client you need to see, and start prioritizing.

You know that one client really keen on your product and is ready to buy, so you prioritize them with an "A" - this is a prospect that's really worth focusing on. Conversely, you know that another prospect is playing you off against several competitors, meaning that the you'll make less profit, and that there's a reasonable chance that you won't get the business. You prioritize this person with a "D". It's worth making some effort here, but you should focus most of your attention on better prospects.

Reference:
James Manktelow & Amy Carlson.

THE AUTHOR

Dr. Sahadeva dasa (Sanjay Shah) is a monk in vaisnava tradition. His areas of work include research in Vedic and contemporary thought, Corporate and educational training, social work and counselling, travelling, writing books and of course, practicing spiritual life and spreading awareness about the same.

He is also an accomplished musician, composer, singer, instruments player and sound engineer. He has more than a dozen albums to his credit so far. (SoulMelodies.com)

His varied interests include alternative holistic living, Vedic studies, social criticism, environment, linguistics, history, art & crafts, nature studies, web technologies etc.

Many of his books have been acclaimed internationally and translated in other languages.

By The Same Author

Oil-Final Countdown To A Global Crisis And Its Solutions

End of Modern Civilization And Alternative Future

To Kill Cow Means To End Human Civilization

Cow And Humanity - Made For Each Other

Cows Are Cool - Love 'Em!

Let's Be Friends - A Curious, Calm Cow

Wondrous Glories of Vraja

We Feel Just Like You Do

Tsunami Of Diseases Headed Our Way - Know Your Food Before Time Runs Out

Cow Killing And Beef Export - The Master Plan To Turn India Into A Desert

By 2050

Capitalism Communism And Cowism - A New Economics For The 21st Century

Noble Cow - Munching Grass, Looking Curious And Just Hanging Around

World - Through The Eyes Of Scriptures

An Inch of Time Can Not Be Bought With A Mile of Gold

Life Is Nothing But Time - Time Is Life, Life Is Time

Lost Time Is Never Found Again

Spare Us Some Carcasses - An Appeal From The Vultures

Cow Dung - A Down-To- Earth Solution To Global Warming And Climate

Change

Cow Dung For Food Security And Survival of Human Race

(More information on availability on DrDasa.com)

www.ingramcontent.com/pod-product-compliance
Lightning Source LLC
Chambersburg PA
CBHW060524030426
42337CB00015B/1987